Reach
HIGHER

Program Authors

Nancy Frey

Lada Kratky

Nonie K. Lesaux

Sylvia Linan-Thompson

Deborah J. Short

Jennifer D. Turner

NATIONAL GEOGRAPHIC
LEARNING

Australia · Brazil · Mexico · Singapore · United Kingdom · United States

NATIONAL GEOGRAPHIC
L E A R N I N G

National Geographic Learning,
a Cengage Company

Reach Higher 3A
Program Authors: Nancy Frey, Lada Kratky,
Nonie K. Lesaux, Sylvia Linan-Thompson,
Deborah J. Short, Jennifer D. Turner

Publisher, English Medium Instruction (EMI):
Erik Gundersen

Associate Director, R&D: Barnaby Pelter

Senior Development Editors:
Jacqueline Eu

Ranjini Fonseka

Kelsey Zhang

Director of Global Marketing: Ian Martin

Heads of Regional Marketing:
Charlotte Ellis (Europe, Middle East and Africa)

Kiel Hamm (Asia)

Irina Pereyra (Latin America)

Product Marketing Manager: David Spain

Senior Production Controller: Tan Jin Hock

Senior Media Researcher (Covers): Leila Hishmeh

Senior Designer: Lisa Trager

Director, Operations: Jason Seigel

Operations Support:
Rebecca Barbush

Drew Robertson

Caroline Stephenson

Nicholas Yeaton

Manufacturing Planner: Mary Beth Hennebury

Publishing Consultancy and Composition:
MPS North America LLC

For permission to use material from this text or product,
submit all requests online at **cengage.com/permissions**
Further permissions questions can be emailed to
permissionrequest@cengage.com

ISBN-13: 978-0-357-36687-5

National Geographic Learning
20 Channel Center Street
Boston, MA 02210
USA

Locate your local office at **international.cengage.com/region**

Visit National Geographic Learning online at **ELTNGL.com**
Visit our corporate website at **www.cengage.com**

Printed in China
Print Number: 08   Print Year: 2024

Contents at a Glance

Table of Contents

Happy to Help

Unit 1

Extra phonics support with **READ ON YOUR OWN**

Helping Hands

SOCIAL STUDIES
▸ Individual Actions

A World of Ideas

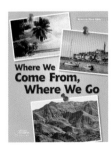

Where We Come From Where We Go

Table of Contents

Nature's Balance

(?) BIG QUESTION

What happens when nature loses its balance?

Extra phonics support with **READ ON YOUR OWN**

 **Look-Alikes**

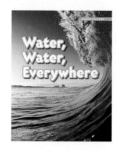 **Water, Water, Everywhere**

SCIENCE

▸ Ecosystems

A Good Cause

Table of Contents

Life in the Soil

Unit 3

(?) BIG QUESTION

What is so amazing about plants?

Part 1

Extra phonics support with **READ ON YOUR OWN**

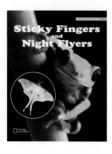

**Sticky Fingers and
Night Flyers**

SCIENCE
▸ Plant Life Cycles
▸ Plant Diversity

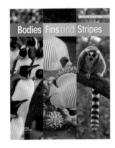

Bodies Fins and Stripes

Table of Contents

Let's Work Together

Unit 4

? BIG QUESTION

What's the best way to get things done?

Part 1

Extra phonics support with **READ ON YOUR OWN**

**National
Treasures**

SOCIAL STUDIES

▸ Community

**Raining Cats
and Dogs**

Genres at a Glance

Happy to Help

? BIG Question

How do people help each other?

ABU DHABI, United Arab Emirates
A teacher guiding a student with special needs to complete a task

Unit at a Glance
▷ **Language Focus**: Retell a Story, Make Comparisons
▷ **Reading Strategy**: Preview and Predict, Monitor and Clarify
▷ **Phonics Focus**: Compound Words, Syllable Division
▷ **Topic**: Helping

Share What You Know

Do It!

❶ **Think** about the people you know. Who could use some help?

❷ **Draw** yourself helping the person.

❸ **Tell** the class your idea. How does it make you feel?

I can read to my little sister.

Retell a Story

Listen to Tanya's story. Then listen to her friend Sonia retell the story. Use **Language Frames** to tell a new story. Have a partner retell the story to you.

A Friend Helps Out

Tanya:
The day my puppy ran away
I searched everywhere.
Sonia helped me find him.
He was right under the stairs.

Sonia:
First, the puppy ran away.
Next, Tanya searched around.
Then, I came by to help my friend.
Finally, the pup was found!

Chant

Key Words

action

difference

gift

problem

receive

solution

🔊 Key Words

Look at the pictures. Use **Key Words** and other words to talk about **actions** that make a **difference**.

Friends see the **problem**.

They have a **solution**. They fix the house.

A Gift of Kindness

Thank you!

She **received** help from her friends.

Talk Together

Think of a time when you helped someone in your community. Use **Language Frames** from page 4 and **Key Words** to retell the story.

5

Plot

When you tell a story, you tell the events in order.

- The **beginning** is what happens first.
- The **middle** is what happens next.
- The **end** is what happens last.

All these events are called the **plot**.

Look at these pictures. They tell a story about Tanya.

Map and Talk

You can use a story map to show the plot of a story. Here's how you make one.

The **beginning** goes in the first box. The **middle** goes in the second box. The **end** goes in the last box.

Story Map

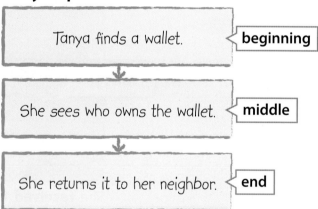

Talk Together

Tell a partner a story about someone you know who needs help. Your partner makes a story map.

◀) More Key Words

Use these words to talk about "Those Shoes" and "Guardian Angel."

kindness
noun

You show **kindness** when you are nice to someone. Teddy shows **kindness** to his mom.

need
verb

When you **need** something, you cannot live without it. People **need** to drink water.

understand
verb

When you **understand** something, you know what it means. Now he **understands** his homework.

value
verb

When you **value** something, you care about it. The girl loves and **values** her dog.

want
verb

To **want** something is to hope or wish for it. He **wants** to get a guitar like this one.

Talk Together

Make a Vocabulary Example Chart for the **Key Words**. Then compare your chart with a partner's.

Word	Definition	Example
Kindness	a nice act	My friend helped me fix my bike.

7

Learn to Preview and Predict

Look at the picture. The text does not say how Tanya will help, but you can look for details in the picture. This is called **previewing**. Then you can make a guess about what will happen next. This is called **predicting**.

When you read a text, you can **preview** and **predict**. This helps you decide on a purpose for reading.

How to Preview and Predict

👁	**1.** Read the title. Look at the pictures. Think about what you will read.	I read _____ . I see _____ .
💭	**2.** Make predictions as you read.	I predict _____ .
👁	**3.** Read on to check whether your predictions are correct or incorrect.	My prediction _____ .

Talk Together

Read Tanya's story. Read the sample prediction. Then use **Language Frames** to make and confirm predictions. Tell a partner about them.

Story

A Puppy Problem

I **received** a puppy for my birthday. It was the **gift** I really **wanted**. I named him Riley.

Riley was almost perfect. He was always happy, and he barked all the time. There was just one **problem** about that.

Our neighbor Mrs. Perry said that Riley was too loud. I didn't **understand**. All puppies bark. Right?

Mom said, "Mrs. Perry **needs** rest and quiet. I really **value** her friendship. Let's teach Riley not to bark so much." Then we took Riley to doggy school. He was in a class with many other puppies. ◀

In just a few weeks, Riley learned not to bark so much. That made a big **difference**.

Riley and I went to visit Mrs. Perry. "Thank you for your **Kindness**," she told me. She gave Riley a pat on the head. Now she really likes my puppy, too! ◀

Sample Prediction

"I read the title. I see a puppy in a box.

I predict that someone gets a puppy.

My prediction is correct. Tanya gets a puppy."

◀ = A good place to make a prediction

9

Compound Words

goldfish

sailboat

Listen and Learn

Listen to the compound words that name the pictures. Match the two smaller words that make up each picture word.

1.

back	boy
note	pack
paper	pad

2.

smile	shine
flash	might
star	light

3.

back	fire
bag	mark
camp	room

4.

hand	bag
milk	shelf
book	shake

🔊 Listen and read. Find the compound words.

Making a Difference

There are people everywhere who make a difference. Their actions solve problems and help others. Firefighters are an example. They put out fires and save people.

Many people show kindness to others. Some help build playgrounds for children. Others help out at school. They help keep the classroom neat. They clean the whiteboards. They even help clean the playground. Sometimes just a kind word is a great gift.

How can you make a difference? First, think about your community. Does it need a cleanup? Are there people in need of help? Next, think about what you can do. Then, decide whether you need others to help you. Finally, get busy and make someone's life brighter.

Work with a partner.
Take turns. One partner should say a compound word from the passage. The other should find the word and say it again. Then switch roles and say another word.

◄ Practice reading compound words by reading "Making a Difference" with a partner.

11

Read a Story

Genre

A story that tells about events that could really happen is **realistic fiction**.

Characters

Characters are the people in the story. This story is told by a character named Jeremy. He uses words like *I, me,* and *my* to tell his story.

Jeremy

Grandma

Antonio

Those Shoes

by **Maribeth Boelts**

illustrated by **Noah Z. Jones**

I have dreams about those shoes. Black **high-tops**. Two white stripes.

"Grandma, I **want** them."

"There's no room for 'want' around here," Grandma says. "What you *need* are new boots for winter."

◀ **high-tops** sports shoes

Brandon T. comes to school in those shoes. He says he's the fastest runner now, not me. I was always the fastest runner before **those shoes came along**.

Next, Allen, Jacob, and Terrence **each get a pair**.

those shoes came along Brandon T. got those shoes

each get a pair get the same shoes

Then one day, in the middle of kickball, one of my shoes **comes apart**.

"Looks like you could use a new pair, Jeremy," Mr. Alfrey, the **guidance counselor**, says. He gives me a pair of shoes with a cartoon animal on it.

comes apart tears, rips
guidance counselor an adult who helps students solve **problems**

When I come back to the classroom, the only kid
not laughing is Antonio Parker.

At home, Grandma says, "How kind of Mr. Alfrey."
I nod and **turn my back**. I'm not going to cry about
any dumb shoes.

---

turn my back turn away

▶ **Before You Continue**
1. **Clarify** Why can't Jeremy get the new shoes he **wants**?
2. **Character's Motive** Why does Jeremy want the black high-tops?

▶ **Predict**
What will Jeremy do to get the
new black shoes?

On Saturday Grandma says, "Let's **check out** those shoes you're **wanting** so much. I got a little bit of money **set aside**. It might be enough—**you never know**."

check out look at
set aside saved
you never know you might be surprised

At the shoe store, Grandma turns over the shoes that Jeremy **wants** . She **checks the price**. When she sees it, she sits down **heavily**.

"Maybe they wrote it down wrong," I say.

Grandma shakes her head.

checks the price looks to see how much the shoes cost

heavily in a sad way

Then I remember the **thrift shops**. We ride
the bus to the first one. There's every kind of shoe
except the ones I **want**.

We ride the bus to the second thrift shop. Not a
pair of those shoes **in sight**.

thrift shops stores that sell used clothes
and shoes

except the ones but not the shoes

in sight anywhere

Around the corner is the third thrift shop. I see something in the window.

I shove my foot into the first shoe. Grandma feels for my toes at the end of the shoe.

"Oh, Jeremy," she says. "I can't **spend good money** on shoes that **don't fit**."

"They're okay," I say, curling my toes. Then I buy them with my own money.

spend good money use money
I worked so hard to save
don't fit are too small

A few days later, Grandma puts a new pair of snow boots in my closet. She doesn't say a word about my **too-big feet shuffling around in my too-small shoes**.

"Sometimes shoes **stretch**," I say.

too-big feet shuffling around in my too-small shoes shoes that are too small for my feet

stretch get bigger

▶ **Before You Continue**

1. **Confirm Prediction** What **actions** did Jeremy take to get the black shoes? Was your prediction correct?

2. **Character** How do Jeremy's actions show what kind of person he is?

▶ **Predict**
What will Jeremy do with the
too-small shoes?

I check every day, but those shoes don't stretch. I
have to wear **my Mr. Alfreys** instead.

One day during Math, I **glance** at Antonio's
shoes. One of them is **taped up**, and his feet look
smaller than mine.

my Mr. Alfreys the shoes Mr. Alfrey gave me
glance look quickly
taped up held together with tape

I'm not going to do it!

That night, I am awake for a long time thinking about Antonio.

When morning comes, I run across the street to Antonio's apartment. I put the shoes in front of his door. I push the doorbell—and run.

At school, I feel happy when I look at
Antonio's face and mad when I look at my
Mr. Alfrey shoes.

Later, snow is everywhere.
Then I remember what I have in my
backpack. New black boots.

Standing in line to go to recess, Antonio
leans forward.

"Thanks," he says.

I smile and give him a **nudge**. "Let's race!" ❖

nudge friendly push

▶ **Before You Continue**

1. **Confirm Prediction** What did you think
   Jeremy would do with the small shoes?
   Was your prediction correct?
2. **Character** How does Jeremy feel about
   helping Antonio? How do you know?

Think and Respond

Talk About It

1. Name two **realistic** events that happen in the story.

   One realistic event in the story is _____ .

   _____ was also like real life.

2. How would Antonio retell this story? Work with a partner to **retell the story** as if you are Antonio.

   First, _____ . Next, _____ . Then, _____ . Finally, _____ .

3. Compare how Jeremy feels about the black high-tops and the shoes from Mr. Alfrey. Which does he **want**? Which does he **need**? Why?

   Jeremy wants _____ , because _____ .

   Jeremy needs _____ , because _____ .

Write About It

Imagine you are Antonio. Write a sentence to tell how you felt when you **received** Jeremy's **gift**. Use **Key Words**.

When Jeremy gave me the shoes, I felt _____ because _____ .

Plot

The events of a story are called the **plot**. Create a story map to show the main events in "Those Shoes."

Story Map

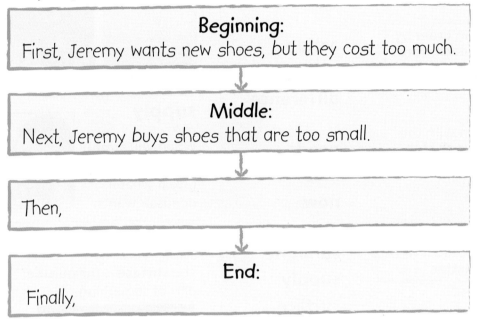

> **Beginning:**
> First, Jeremy wants new shoes, but they cost too much.

> **Middle:**
> Next, Jeremy buys shoes that are too small.

> Then,

> **End:**
> Finally,

Now use your story map to sequence and summarize the plot's main events for a partner. Use time-order words and **Key Words**. Record your summary.

> First, _____ .
> Next, _____ .
> Then, _____ .
> Finally, _____ .

Fluency

Practice reading with expression. Rate your reading.

Talk Together

How can one act of **kindness** make a **difference**? Draw a picture. Use **Key Words** to tell your class about the picture.

Word Work

Alphabetical Order

The words in a dictionary follow the same order as the letters of the alphabet. To look up words, you need to know **alphabetical order**.

> These words are in order by the first letter of each word.

<u>a</u>ction
<u>c</u>hange
<u>d</u>ifference

> If the words begin with the same first letter, look at the second letter.

n<u>e</u>ed
n<u>i</u>ce
n<u>o</u>w

> If the words begin with the same first and second letters, look at the third letter.

su<u>n</u>light
su<u>p</u>ply
su<u>r</u>face

sunlight
noun
Sunlight is the light that comes from the sun.

day

night

supply
verb
When you **supply** something, you give It what it needs or wants.

surface
noun
The **surface** is the outside part of something.

the surface of the Moon

Try It Together

Answer the questions.

1. **Which word comes before want in a dictionary?**

   A **w**ait

   B **w**hat

   C **w**ave

   D **w**ater

2. **Which word comes after receive in a dictionary?**

   A **r**ace

   B **r**ead

   C **r**ealistic

   D **r**estaurant

Guardian Angel

by **Francisco X. Alarcón**

illustrated by **Josée Masse**

when I felt so sad
and all alone

wanting to cry
in the classroom

Guardian Angel A kind, helpful person

▸ **Before You Continue**
1. **Ask Questions** What questions do you have about the speaker of the poem?
2. **Predict** What do you think will happen to help the speaker feel better?

the girl seated
next to me

suddenly
held my hand

suddenly quickly,
unexpectedly

and with the darkest
and **most tender** eyes

I have ever seen—
told me **without a word**:

"**don't worry**
you're not alone" ❖

most tender kindest
without a word without talking
don't worry do not feel sad

▶ **Before You Continue**
1. **Confirm Prediction** What happened to change the speaker's feelings?
2. **Character** What is the girl like? How do her **actions** help the speaker?

Compare Genres

Key Words

action	receive
difference	solution
gift	understand
kindness	value
need	want
problem	

A story like "Those Shoes" and a lyrical poem like "Guardian Angel" are different forms of writing, or genres. How are the two genres different? How are they the same? Work with a partner to complete the checklist chart.

Checklist Chart

> Think about each characteristic.

	Story	Poem
It is arranged in lines.		✔
It has paragraphs.	✔	
It is usually long.		
It is usually short.		
It expresses the writer's feelings.		
The words sound like music.		

> Write check marks to show whether the characteristics describe a story, a poem, or both.

Talk Together

How do people help each other? Think about the characters in the story and the poem. How do their **actions** help others? Use **Key Words** to talk about your ideas.

Complete Sentences

A sentence expresses a complete thought. A **complete sentence** has two parts.

Grammar Rules Complete Sentences

• The <u>subject</u> tells whom or what the sentence is about.	<u>Grandma</u> <u>The boys</u>
• The <u>predicate</u> tells what the subject is, has, or does.	<u>shakes her head</u> <u>want those shoes</u>
• To make a complete sentence, use both a <u>subject</u> and a <u>predicate</u>.	<u>Grandma</u> <u>shakes her head</u>. <u>The boys</u> <u>want those shoes</u>.

Read Sentences

Read this passage from "Those Shoes." Which group of words is a complete sentence?

> I have dreams about those shoes. Black high-tops.
> Two white stripes.

Write Sentences

Choose a picture from pages 4–7. Write a sentence to tell what is happening. Be sure to include a subject and a predicate. Read your sentence to a partner.

Language Frames

- Before, _____ was
  _____ .
- Now, it is _____ .

Make Comparisons

Listen to Kemal's song. Then use **Language Frames** to tell how you changed something that helped other people.

I Am Feeling Good

Song

I am feeling good.
I have helped to clean my street.
First, I picked up all the trash,
Then I gave it a good sweep.
Oh, before, the street was messy,
But now, it is clean and neat.
And I'm feeling good!

Tune: "Do Your Ears Hang Low?"

Key Words
improve
individual
neighborhood
offer
volunteer

🔊 Key Words

Look at the graphic organizer to learn **Key Words**.

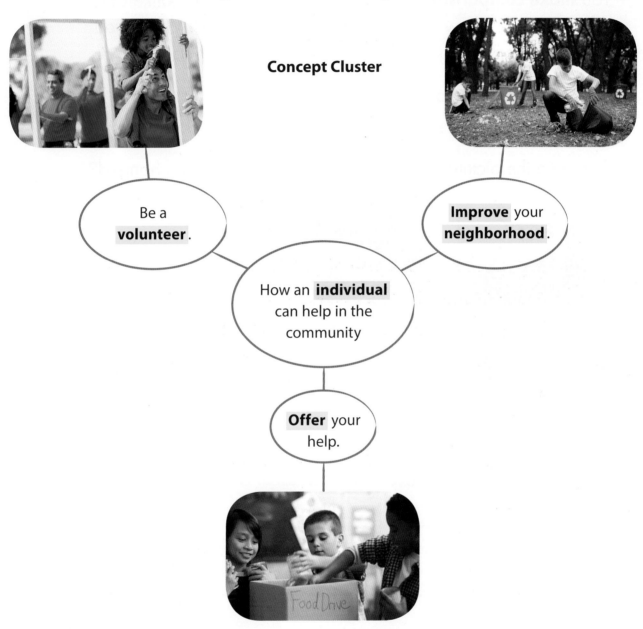

Concept Cluster

Be a **volunteer**.

Improve your **neighborhood**.

How an **individual** can help in the community

Offer your help.

Talk Together

How have you helped in your community? How did things change? Try to use **Language Frames** from page 36 and **Key Words** to make comparisons for a partner.

37

Make Comparisons

You **make comparisons** to show how two things are alike or different, or to show how something has changed. When you talk about something that has changed over time, use:

- *before* and *then* to tell about the past
- *now* and *after* to tell about the present

Compare the pictures. How has the area near the tree changed?

Map and Talk

You can make a comparison chart to show how something has changed.

Comparison Chart

Before	Now
There were weeds and trash around the tree.	There are flowers around the tree.

Talk Together

Tell a partner about something that has improved. Tell what it was like before and what it is like now. Your partner makes a comparison chart.

🔊 More Key Words

Use these words to talk about "The World's Greatest Underachiever" and "Joseph Lekuton: Making a Difference."

benefit
noun

A **benefit** is something that is helpful. One **benefit** of rain is that it helps plants grow tall.

duty
noun

When you do your **duty**, you do what you are supposed to do.

identify
verb

When you **identify** something, you tell what it is. She wants to **identify** a type of bird.

impact
noun

What you do has an **impact** on things. The children have a positive **impact** on the park.

learn
verb

To **learn** means to find out how to do something. You can **learn** to play music.

Talk Together

Make a Study Card for each **Key Word**. Then compare your cards with a partner's.

> learn
>
> **What it means:** to find out
>
> **Example:** I learn about horses from my uncle.
>
> **Not an example:** I don't know anything about dogs.

Learn to Monitor and Clarify

Look at the round picture of Kemal and his friend. Ask yourself a question about what you see. To find the answer, look more closely at the round picture or look at the big picture.

When you read, check or **monitor** yourself to make sure you understand everything. Ask questions to **clarify** the parts you do not understand.

How to Monitor and Clarify

👁	**1.** Read the text carefully.	I read _____ .
?	**2.** Ask yourself: What does this mean?	I ask myself: _____ ?
👁	**3.** Reread the text or read on. Look for facts and details to answer your questions.	I find out _____ .

Talk Together

Read Kemal's letter with a partner. Read the sample. Then use **Language Frames** to monitor and clarify. Tell your partner how you checked your understanding of the text.

Letter

March 14, 20__

Dear Opal,

This week I **learned** something important. I learned that one **individual** can make a big difference. Let me tell you how.

It had *been* raining hard all week. Then last night, it became a flood. Mr. Ruiz **identified** the problem right away. The flood wall in our **neighborhood** was about to burst! Everyone started to fill and stack sandbags. But the water was rising fast. More **volunteers** were needed, so I **offered** to help.

We stacked hundreds of sandbags. But the situation didn't **improve**. The water kept going higher and higher. Nobody gave up, though. We all did our **duty** and kept working hard.

Finally, the rain stopped. We all cheered. Our neighborhood was saved!

Boy, was I tired, but I felt good, too. My help made an **impact**, and we all understood the **benefit** of working together.

Your friend,

Kemal

Sample

"I read that Kemal learned something.

I ask myself: What did he learn?

I find out that he learned something because of a flood."

◀ = A good place to monitor and clarify your reading

41

🔊 Syllable Division

cat = cat =
1 syllable

rabbit = rab/bit =
2 syllables

puppy = pup/py =
2 syllables

Listen and **Learn**

🔊 Listen to each sentence. Choose the answer that shows the correct way to divide the word into syllables.

1. You should wear a **helmet** when you ride your bike.

he/lmet   hel/met   helm/et

2. A **magnet** attracts things that are metal.

mag/net   ma/gnet   magn/et

3. We read a story about a **princess** locked in a castle.

pri/ncess   princ/ess
prin/cess

4. He drove the **tractor** into the field.

tract/or   trac/tor   tra/ctor

🔊 Listen and read. Find one-syllable words with the consonant-vowel-consonant (CVC) pattern and two-syllable words with the vowel-consonant-consonant-vowel pattern (VCCV).

A Neighborhood Cleanup

These kids are upset about the environment. There is too much trash everywhere. The kids decided that they could have an impact on the problem. They start in their own neighborhood.

The kids picked a date for a cleanup. They asked people to volunteer. They asked shop owners for help. Some gave garbage bags, gloves, and tools. One shop offered snacks for the workers. A garden shop offered free plants.

The kids were very happy. Before the cleanup, their neighborhood was filled with rubbish. Now it was beautiful. The kids learned the benefit of working together. They were able to improve their community. They had a small, but important, impact on their world.

Work with a partner.

Take turns. Point to a word with one of the syllable patterns in this lesson. Have your partner tell if it is a one-syllable word or a two syllable word. Then switch roles and pick another word.

◀ Practice reading words with consonant-vowel-consonant (CVC) syllables and vowel-consonant-consonant-vowel (VCCV) syllables by reading "A Neighborhood Cleanup" with a partner.

Read an Autobiography

Genre

An **autobiography** is the true story of a person's life written by that person.

First-Person Narrator

The person who tells the story is the narrator. A first-person narrator uses first-person words to tell what happens to him or her.

> **I** studied **my** spelling words in my apartment in New York City. Somehow, during the time it took **me** to walk the block from my apartment to my school, the words vanished.

The World's GREATEST Underachiever

BY HENRY WINKLER

HENRY WINKLER is best known for **playing** "The Fonz" on the TV show *Happy Days*. Today, he **is the co-author of a series** of children's books. Winkler also visits schools to talk to students and share his story.

▲ Winkler is an actor, director, producer, and co-author of children's books.

◀ Winkler when he was nine years old

playing being a character called
is the co-author of a series works with another person to write a group

▶ **Set a Purpose**
Henry has trouble in school.
Find out what the problem is.

All through grade school, I **was tutored**. If I got a D, I was **in heaven**. If I got a C-minus, I had **achieved greatness**. A's and B's were a **kingdom I could never enter**.

▲ Winkler with his classmates at school

was tutored got extra help with schoolwork
in heaven very happy
achieved greatness done a great job
kingdom I could never enter goal I could
  never reach

I studied my spelling words in my apartment in New York City. Somehow, during the time it took me to walk the block from my apartment to my school, the words **vanished**.

vanished disappeared

My teacher, Miss Adolf, had given me a list of ten spelling words.

My mother and I **went over** the list until I *knew* those words. I felt **terrific**. I thought, *Wow! This time, I'm going to* **pass**.

went over studied
terrific great
pass get a good grade

▶ **Before You Continue**

1. **Clarify** What does Henry mean when he says "the words vanished?" How is this a problem at school?
2. **Point of View** Who is telling the story? How do you know?

Henry studied his spelling words.
Will his spelling **improve** on the test?

The next day, I went into the classroom and took out a sheet of paper. Then Miss Adolf gave us the words. The first word was *carpet*. I wrote that one down: *c-a-r-p-e-t*. I was feeling **pretty confident**.

▲ **A school in New York City**

pretty confident sure that I would do well

Then came *neighbor*–I wrote down the letter *n*. Then *rhythm*–I knew there was an *r*. *Suburban*–I wrote *s-u-b*.

My heart sank. I had gone from **100 percent to maybe a D-minus**. Where did the words go?

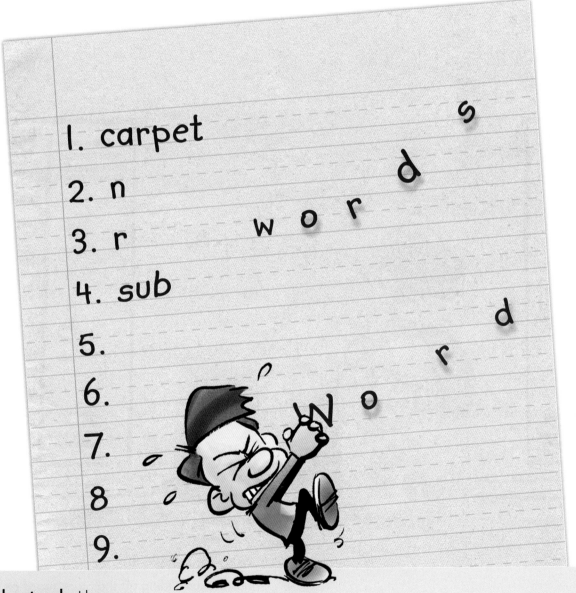

1. carpet
2. n
3. r
4. sub
5.
6.
7.
8.
9.

words
words
words

My heart sank. I became very unhappy.

100 percent to maybe a D-minus good to bad

Some people talk about **information sliding off the blackboard of your brain.** That was my life. I was called "stupid," "lazy." **My self-image was down around my ankles**.

information sliding off the blackboard of your brain forgetting things you know

My self-image was down around my ankles. I did not feel good about myself.

The one thing **I had going for me** was my **sense of humor**. It sure didn't get me any A's, though. It got me a trip to the principal's office.

No matter what I did, it didn't seem to **make a difference**.

I had going for me that helped
sense of humor way of making people laugh
make a difference help

▶ Before You Continue
1. **Confirm Prediction** Did Henry's spelling **improve** on the test? Explain.
2. **Goal/Outcome** What does Henry want?

▮ wish I'd known then what I know now: I have
dyslexia. My brain learns differently. When my
stepson, Jed, was in the third grade, we had him tested
for learning differences. As they explained dyslexia to
him, I thought, *That's me!*

▼ **A person with dyslexia might see**
the **as** *teh.* **He or she might see** *was* **as**
saw, **and** *bird* **as** *brid.*

The owl was a bird.

Teh owl saw a ⨉ brid.

The owl was

dyslexia a learning problem that makes it hard
to read, spell, write, and do math

A learning disability can really **affect** the way you feel about yourself. Now I know that even if a person **learns** differently, he or she can still **be filled with greatness**.

▼ Winkler became famous when he grew up. Here he is as *"The Fonz."*

affect change
be filled with greatness do wonderful things

Today when I visit schools, I tell children that everyone has something special **inside**. It's our job to **figure out what that is**. Dig deep, get it out, and give it to the world as a gift. ❖

▲ Winkler helps young people. He shares his story with them.

inside that people cannot always see at first

figure out what that is find what makes us special and great

▶ **Before You Continue**

1. **Confirm Prediction** How does Henry **learn** to feel good about himself? Was your prediction correct?

2. **Goal/Outcome** What goal does Henry have for the young people he meets today?

Henry Winkler

Even though school was hard for him, Henry Winkler graduated from high school. He then went on to college and got a master's degree in drama from Yale University.

Mr. Winkler's difficulties in school inspired him to write. His popular children's books are about a character named Hank Zipzer. Like Mr. Winkler, Hank has a learning disability. In his stories, Mr. Winkler uses the real names of two teachers. One of them is Miss Adolf!

Winkler with some of his Hank Zipzer books ▶

Writing Tip ✏

Henry Winkler uses words that sound like him. He writes using his own voice. Write a sentence to describe how you feel about going to school. Use words that sound like you. Read the sentence aloud. Does it sound like something you would say?

Think and Respond

Key Words	
benefit	individual
duty	learn
identify	neighborhood
impact	offer
improve	volunteer

Talk About It

1. How do you know that "The World's Greatest Underachiever" is an **autobiography**?

I know that it is an autobiography because _____ .

2. Compare how the author felt about himself when he was young to how he feels now.

Before, Henry felt _____ .

Now, he feels _____ because _____ .

3. Why do you think Henry calls himself an underachiever in school?

Henry calls himself an underachiever because _____ .

Write About It

Henry helps children. Write a letter thanking him. Tell him what you **learned** from his story. Then share how you can have a positive **impact** on people's lives. Use **Key Words**.

_____ , 20_____

Dear Mr. Winkler,

Thank you _____ . I learned _____ .

Your friend,

_____

Make Comparisons

Create a comparison chart to show how Henry changed in "The World's Greatest Underachiever."

Comparison Chart

Before	Now
1. Henry had trouble spelling.	1. He writes books.
2. He didn't like school.	2.

Use your comparison chart to compare things about Henry's story for a partner. Use the sentence frames and **Key Words**. Record your discussion.

> Before, Henry _____ .
> Now, he _____ .

Fluency

Practice reading with intonation. Rate your reading.

Talk Together

How many ways do adults help students in school? With a partner, brainstorm a list. Use **Key Words**. Share your list with the class.

Determine Meanings

When you read an unknown word, you can find its meaning in a dictionary or glossary. In a dictionary, words are listed in alphabetical order.

Look at the following example of a dictionary entry.

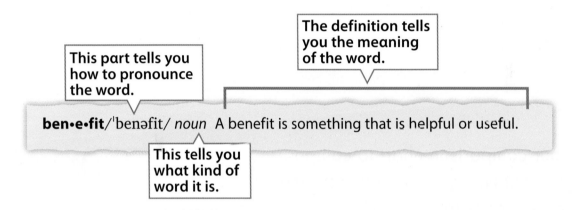

The definition tells you the meaning of the word.

This part tells you how to pronounce the word.

ben•e•fit/ˈbenəfit/ *noun* A benefit is something that is helpful or useful.

This tells you what kind of word it is.

Try It Together

Use the dictionary entries to answer the questions.

im•prove *verb* To improve something is to make it better.
in•di•vid•u•al *noun* An individual is one person.

1. What kind of word is improve?

 A verb

 B noun

 C adverb

 D adjective

2. What does individual mean?

 A noun

 B improve

 C something

 D one person

NATIONAL
GEOGRAPHIC
EXCLUSIVE

Making Connections Read about a man who tries to help others in Kenya, Africa.

Genre A **biography** tells the story of someone's life. The author uses words like *he* and *him* to give information about the person.

Joseph Lekuton:
Making a Difference
BY PHILLIP KENNEDY

▲ Joseph Lekuton

Joseph Lekuton was born in Kenya, a country in Africa. Joseph and his family **are Maasai**. Many of the Maasai take care of **cattle**.

Kenya — AFRICA

are Maasai belong to a group of people in Kenya who live and work together

cattle cows

▶ **Before You Continue**

1. **Identify Details** What group does Joseph's family belong to? What work do most of the people do?
2. **Ask Questions** What questions do you have about Joseph?

61

An Important Decision

Every Maasai family has to send one child to school. So Joseph's father sent one of Joseph's brothers. But his brother didn't like school. He hid in a **hyena hole** and didn't go to class!

▲ Lekuton's village

hyena

Decision Choice

◄ **hyena hole** hole where a wild animal called a hyena lives

Joseph wanted to go to school. He volunteered to go instead of his brother. When Joseph was older, he went to schools in far-away parts of the country. One school was **600 miles** away.

▲ **Kenyan children on their way to school**

600 miles very far; about 965 kilometers

▶ **Before You Continue**

1. **Clarify** Find sentences that tell you that Joseph wanted to go to school and his brother did not.

2. **Point of View** Does the author tell the story or does Joseph? How do you know?

A Challenge

Keeping Joseph in school was **difficult**. His family sold a lot of their cattle to pay **his school fees**. Joseph was also far from home. He couldn't always help his family care for their cattle.

▲ **A Maasai boy takes care of cattle.**

Challenge Hard Job
difficult not easy
his school fees the money it
cost to go to school

A Way to Help Others

When Joseph grew up, he became a teacher. He helped build schools in Maasai communities. He also **helped create scholarships**. Joseph's work has made a difference. Now it is a little easier for Maasai children to go to school.

"The more children we can **educate**, the fewer problems we'll have in Africa," Joseph says. ❖

▲ A school in Kenya

helped create scholarships
   made it possible for more
   children to go to school

educate teach

▶ **Before You Continue**

1. **Make Comparisons** What was Joseph's life like before he went away to school? How did it change after he went to school?

2. **Details** How has Joseph helped to **improve** his community?

Compare Points of View

An autobiography and a biography have different points of view. A point of view is the way a story is told. Who tells the story in an autobiography? Who is the narrator in a biography?

Look at the beginnings of the selections.

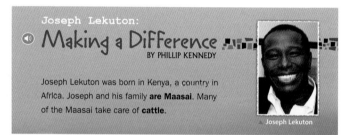

Now write the name of each author next to the correct description below. Then explain to a partner the difference in point of view between a biography and an autobiography.

Tells the story of his or her own life: _____

Tells the story of another person's life: _____

Talk Together

How do people help each other? Think about the people in the autobiography and the biography. How do they help others? Use **Key Words** to talk about your ideas.

More Subjects and Predicates

The **verb**, which is the most important word in the predicate, must agree with the subject of the sentence.

Grammar Rules Subject-Verb Agreement

Verbs in the Present	
• Use -**s** at the end of an action verb if the subject is **he**, **she**, or **it**.	Henry **reads** a spelling word. He **reads** a spelling word.
• Do not use -**s** for **I**, **you**, **we**, and **they**.	The words **slide** off his brain. They **slide** off his brain.
• Use **am** for **I**.	I **am** a fan of Hank Zipzer.
• Use **is** for **he**, **she**, and **it**.	He **is** a funny character.
• Use **are** for **you**, **we**, and **they**.	The books **are** in the library. They **are** in the library.

Read Sentences

Read these sentences from "The World's Greatest Underachiever." Identify the subjects and the verbs.

Today, he is the co-author of a series of children's books. Winkler also visits schools.

Write Sentences

Write two sentences about Henry Winkler. Make sure the subjects and verbs agree. Read your sentences to a partner.

Write About Yourself

Write a Personal Narrative ✏️

Tell about a time when someone in your school helped you, or when you helped someone. You can add your story to a class book.

Study a Model

A personal narrative is a true story. The author uses words like *I*, *me*, and *my*.

The **beginning** tells what the narrative is about.

Open House

by Emilio Campos

Last August, I was a student guide for an open house at my school. My job was to help new students and their parents get used to our school. I handed out school maps and answered questions.

When I saw a mom and her son looking nervous and confused, I went up to help them. The mom started talking in Spanish. Emilio to the rescue! I'm Mexican, so I said in Spanish that I'd show them around.

The **middle** tells more about the event. The author uses an informal style and words that sound like him.

The **end** tells what happened last and why the experience was important.

They both looked so happy! I knew how it felt to be in an unfamiliar place. So, it felt great to help them feel better about being there.

Prewrite

1. **Choose a Topic** What will you write about? Talk with a partner. Choose an event from your life that was important to you.

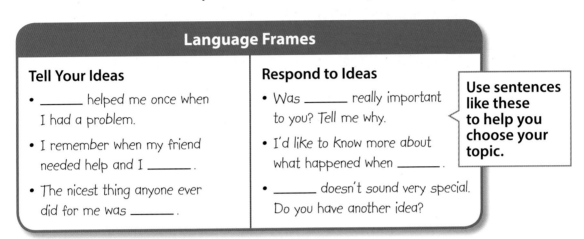

Language Frames

Tell Your Ideas

- _____ helped me once when I had a problem.

- I remember when my friend needed help and I _____ .

- The nicest thing anyone ever did for me was _____ .

Respond to Ideas

- Was _____ really important to you? Tell me why.

- I'd like to know more about what happened when _____ .

- _____ doesn't sound very special. Do you have another idea?

> Use sentences like these to help you choose your topic.

2. **Gather Information** Think about the event. What happened at the beginning, in the middle, and at the end?

3. **Get Organized** Use a story map to help you organize your thoughts.

 Story Map

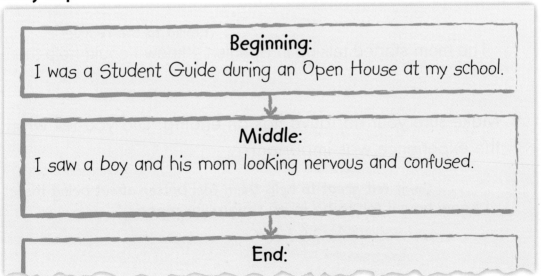

Beginning:
I was a Student Guide during an Open House at my school.

↓

Middle:
I saw a boy and his mom looking nervous and confused.

↓

End:

Draft

Use your story map to write your draft. Use informal words that sound like you. Tell why the experience was important to you.

Revise

1. **Read, Retell, Respond** Read your draft aloud to a partner. Your partner listens and then retells the story. Next, talk about ways to improve your writing.

Language Frames		
Retell • You told me about the time when _____ . • I think this experience was important to you because _____ .	**Make Suggestions** • I'm not sure why _____ was special to you. Can you explain why you chose this topic? • The language is too formal/ informal. Maybe you could change _____ .	**Use sentences like these to respond to your partner's writing.**

2. **Make Changes** Think about your draft and your partner's suggestions. Use revision marks to make your changes.

   • Do your words and sentences sound like you? If not, change some.

   > The mom started talking in Spanish. ~~I knew I could help them.~~ *Emilio to the rescue!*

   • Make sure your narrative has an ending. Did you tell why the experience was important?

   > I knew how it felt to be in an unfamiliar place. *So, it felt great to help them feel better about being there.*

Spelling Tip

✔ When you use the present tense, put **-s** at the end of an action verb if the subject is **he**, **she**, or **it**.

Edit and Proofread

Work with a partner to edit and proofread your personal narrative. Be sure the subject and verb agree in each sentence. Use revision marks to show your changes.

Present

1. **On Your Own** Make a final copy of your personal narrative. Choose a way to share it with your classmates. You might read one another's narratives or sit in a circle and take turns telling your experiences.

Presentation Tips	
If you are the speaker...	**If you are the listener...**
Make eye contact with your listeners. Look up even if you are reading your story.	Nod or smile to show the reader that you are listening attentively.
Keep your expression friendly as you tell about your experience.	Think about why the event was important to the speaker.

2. **In a Group** Collect all the personal narratives. Bind them into a book called "Helping Others." Tell your family and friends about the book. They might want a copy!

Inside the photo:

? BIG Question

How do people help each other?

Talk Together

In this unit, you found lots of answers to the **Big Question**. Now, use your concept map to discuss the **Big Question** with the class.

Concept Map

give others something they need

How people help each other

Write a Plan

Review the ideas on your concept map. Choose your best idea. Then write a plan to tell how you can help others.

Share Your Ideas

Choose one of these ways to share your ideas about the **Big Question**.

Do It!

Draw a Self-Portrait

How do you feel when you do something nice for someone? Draw a picture of yourself to show this feeling. Post your picture in a class Portrait Gallery.

Talk About It!

Form a Panel

With three other classmates, sit in a row of chairs in front of the class. Discuss ways you can help your teachers or other students in school. Afterward, answer questions from the audience.

Write It!

Write a Mini-Biography

Work with a partner. Write about someone you know who has helped others. Tell who the person is and how the person's actions made a difference in other people's lives.

Do It!

Role-Play Workers

Think of workers in your community who help others. Choose a job to role-play. Have your classmates guess your job and tell how you help others.

Nature's Balance

? BIG Question

What happens when nature loses its balance?

THE ARCTIC
Polar bears trying to survive in an environment
damaged by industrial pollution

Unit at a Glance
- **Language Focus:** Ask and Answer Questions, Give and Carry Out Commands
- **Reading Strategy:** Ask Questions
- **Phonics Focus:** Vowel Sounds and Spellings: u_e and oo
- **Topic:** Ecosystems

Share What You Know

Do It!

❶ **Draw** a place where plants and animals live, such as a fish tank or a field.

❷ **Imagine** that something changes in this place. Does the fish tank get dirty? Does rain flood the field?

❸ **Display** your drawing. Tell what could happen to the plants or animals because of the change.

Fish might get sick in dirty water.

Language Focus

Ask and Answer Questions

Listen to the dialogue between Linda and Mike. Then use **Language Frames** with a partner. Ask and answer questions about something in nature.

Dialogue

Key Words

amount

behavior

decrease

increase

supply

🔊 Key Words

Look at this example. Use **Key Words** and other words to talk about bird **behavior**.

What happens when the **supply** of birdseed **increases**?

What happens when the **amount** of birdseed **decreases**?

Talk Together

With a partner, talk about balance and the supply of bird food. Use **Language Frames** from page 76 and **Key Words** to ask and answer questions.

Compare and Contrast

Sometimes you tell how things are alike and how they are different. When you do this, you **compare and contrast**.

Look at the pictures. How are the animals alike and how are they different?

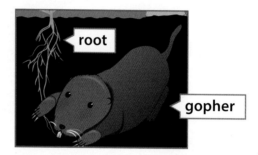

Map and Talk

You can make a Venn diagram to compare and contrast.

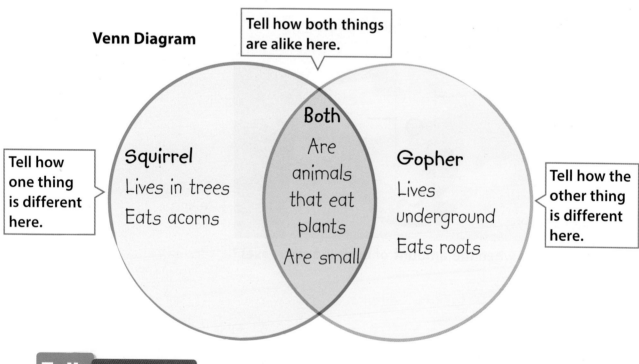

Venn Diagram

Tell how both things are alike here.

Tell how one thing is different here.

Tell how the other thing is different here.

Both
Are animals that eat plants
Are small

Squirrel
Lives in trees
Eats acorns

Gopher
Lives underground
Eats roots

Talk **Together**

Compare and contrast what you see in the pictures on page 77. Tell a partner. Your partner makes a Venn diagram.

🔊 More Key Words

Use these words to talk about "It's All in the Balance" and "Animals, More or Less."

balance
noun

When things are in **balance**, they are even. The two sides of the scale are in **balance**.

control
verb

To **control** means to make a person or thing do what you want. The boys **control** where the car goes.

interact
verb

To **interact** means to act together. The students **interact** with each other to do a science project.

react
verb

When things happen, you usually **react** to them. The child **reacts** to the snowball.

scarce
adjective

When something is **scarce**, it is hard to find or get. Food is **scarce** in this store.

Talk Together

With a partner, take turns telling a story. Use the **Key Words**.

Jim did not control his bike on the hill.

He lost his balance!

Learn to Ask Questions

Look at the picture. Do you understand what Linda and her cat are doing? **Ask** yourself **questions** about what you see. Look more closely at the picture to find the answers.

As you read, **ask questions**. The answers to some questions can be found in the text. Read to find the answers. This will help you understand the text better.

How to Ask Questions

?	**1.** Ask a question.	I wonder: _____ ?
👁	**2.** Look for the answer. You might find the answer in the text. Or you might have to think and search.	I read _____ . So _____ .
💭	**3.** Think about the answer. Read on and ask more questions.	Now I wonder: _____ ?

Language Frames

? I wonder:
_____ ?

👁 I read _____ .
So _____ .

💭 Now I wonder:
_____ ?

Read Linda's fable with a partner. Read the sample questions. Then use **Language Frames** to ask and answer questions to check your understanding.

Fable

The Gopher and the Squirrel

One day Squirrel met Gopher in a garden. She wasn't sure how to **interact** with a gopher. So she spoke politely. "Good day," she said. "May I collect the acorns in this garden?"

"No! Go away!" said Gopher.

This was a rude way to **react** to a polite request. But Squirrel tried again. "You see, the trees didn't get enough rain this year. Nature is out of **balance**. Acorns are **scarce**."

"I can't **control** the weather," said Gopher. "But I control this garden, and all the acorns are mine."

"But you have roots to eat," Squirrel protested.

"So what? The acorns are mine, too!" Gopher replied.

Then Squirrel asked, "Is that little wire shed near the fence yours, too?"

"What little wire shed?" asked Gopher. He came out of his hole to take a look. The shed was just the right size for a gopher. A few carrots were on the floor. Gopher ran inside to get the carrots. Slam! Down fell the cage door. He was trapped.

Squirrel laughed. "Looks like I'm in control now!"

Moral: If you are selfish, you might lose everything.

Sample Questions

"I wonder: Why is Gopher so rude?

I read that Gopher doesn't want to share the acorns. So I know that he is greedy.

Now I wonder: Will Gopher give Squirrel some acorns?"

◄ = A good place to ask a question

🔊 Vowel Sounds and Spellings: *u_e*

flute

tube

Listen and Learn

🔊 Listen to the vowel sound in the picture words. Choose the words that have the same vowel sound.

1.

bone   rude   just

2.

flack   face   tune

3.

more   rule   rake

4.

truce   sprang   tale

Listen and read. Find the words with the vowel sound in *flute* spelled *u_e*.

Over to You

When Nature Loses Its Balance

A healthy habitat must *be* in balance. What does this mean? Here is an example. As a rule, rabbits eat plants. The rabbits keep the plants under control. Foxes eat rabbits. Foxes make sure there are not too many rabbits. The environment is balanced.

A swamp in Florida is an example of a habitat that is not in balance. What is the problem? There are too many large snakes. The snakes are not native to the swamp. Who is responsible? Rude pet owners let their pet snakes loose in the swamp. Their numbers have increased. There are now too many large snakes. They are eating too much of the native wildlife. The snakes eat rabbits, foxes, and other small animals. The result is less food for alligators and big, wild cats. Now all of the wildlife in the swamp is becoming scarce. Trained hunters are trying to get rid of the snakes. But it may *be* too hard. The snakes may elude, or get away from, the hunters.

Work with a partner.
Take turns. Choose a word with the vowel sound you hear in *flute* from the passage. Make up your own sentences using the word.

◀ Practice reading words with the vowel sound in *flute* by reading "When Nature Loses Its Balance" with a partner.

83

Read a Humorous Story

Genre
A **humorous story** has funny characters and events.

Setting
The setting is where and when a story happens.

This story happens in a small village in China.

It's All in the Balance

by **Susan Henderson**

▶ **Set a Purpose**
A visitor sees a village garden.
Find out what he doesn't like
about it.

Once there was a **village** that had a very
beautiful garden. Birds sang, bees buzzed in the
trees, and colorful butterflies flew among the many
bright flowers.

The people in the village were very **proud** of
their garden. They thought it was the most
beautiful garden in all the world.

village small town
bright colorful
proud pleased with

One day, a **visitor** came to the village.

"This is a wonderful garden," he said, "except for all the holes in the leaves of the plants."

"Oh dear," said the villagers. "What can we do to fix the leaves?"

"Listen to me," said the visitor. "For I am the greatest gardener in all the land."

visitor guest

"Caterpillars eat leaves, and caterpillars come from eggs laid by butterflies," said the visitor.

"It's simple. If you **dig out** the butterfly bushes, the butterflies will go away—just like that." And the man **snapped** his fingers.

The villagers nodded their heads. *This visitor must be very wise*, they thought.

dig out remove
snapped made a clicking sound

The villagers picked up their **shovels** and **wheelbarrows** and went to work digging up the garden.

Meanwhile, the butterflies and the birds watched from above. "Oh no!" they cried. "What are the villagers doing to our beautiful garden?"

The visitor looked on, quite satisfied with the villagers' work.

shovels tools for digging
wheelbarrows small carts
Meanwhile While this was happening

▶ **Before You Continue**

1. **Cause/Effect** What does the visitor want to remove from the garden? Why?
2. **Ask Questions** Think about the visitor. Ask yourself a question about the character. Look for the answer as you read.

▶ **Predict**

What do you think will happen if the villagers get rid of the butterfly bushes?

A boy who lived outside the village passed by and saw what was happening. He told the villagers that the butterflies said the visitor's **advice** was silly. He **pleaded with** the villagers not to **get rid of** the butterfly bushes.

"The butterflies help keep this garden **in balance**," said the boy. "Butterflies?" **sneered** the visitor. "What do butterflies know?"

advice recommendation
pleaded with begged
get rid of remove
in balance in harmony
sneered mocked with a smile

"What do butterflies know?" the villagers
repeated. They dug up all the bushes and
laughed at the boy as he sadly walked away.

But the boy **saved** one of the butterfly
bushes and took it back to his home.
The butterflies and the birds, angry
with the villagers, went with him.

saved rescued

Soon, the leaves of the plants in the garden looked **glossy** and green. But there were not as many bees or butterflies and **certainly** not as many caterpillars.

There were not many birds either, but the villagers didn't seem to notice. But the boy from outside the village did.

glossy shiny
certainly definitely

When the visitor returned, he said, "The leaves look much better, but your garden is too colorful. Get rid of some of those flowers."

"TOO colorful?" replied the boy from outside the village. "The bird asks, 'How can a garden be too colorful?'"

"What does a bird know?" asked the villagers, and they dug out most of the flowers.

▶ **Before You Continue**

1. **Confirm Prediction** What has happened to the garden so far? Was your prediction correct?
2. **Details** What does the visitor want the villagers to do next? Why?

▶ **Predict**
How will the villagers feel when
the creatures start to disappear?

Time passed. One day, one
of the villagers noticed that the
beehive in the garden was empty.
All the bees were gone.

"Who took the bees?" he **demanded**.

"Where have all the birds gone?"
asked a woman.

"Where are the butterflies?" asked another.

But there was no answer.

beehive home for bees
demanded asked forcefully

All at once, the garden seemed like a very sad place. There were no butterflies or birds. The bees had all gone, too. The garden had lost all its **residents**—and all its color.

"What have we done?" the villagers cried. "What has happened to our beautiful garden?"

All at once Suddenly

residents creatures who lived in the garden

▶**Before You Continue**

1. **Confirm Prediction** What was your prediction? Was it correct? Explain.
2. **Setting** Describe how the garden was different after the creatures disappeared.

▶ **Predict**

Look at the picture of the boy's garden. How will the villagers get their garden back to the way it was?

One day, one of the villagers **happened upon** the boy's house. There were colorful flowers **everywhere**. He saw bees and butterflies. He heard many birds **singing** from the trees.

"Your garden is beautiful," said the man. "Why isn't our garden like this?" he asked.

"Listen to the bees," said the boy.

happened upon accidentally found
everywhere all over
singing chirping and tweeting

"Bees?" said the man. "What do bees—?" Then suddenly, he stopped. And he listened.

"The bees say, we tried to **control** nature," said the man. "But we've **upset** the **balance**. Digging up the butterfly bushes made the butterflies go away. Without the butterflies, there were no caterpillars. With no caterpillars, the birds had nothing to eat, so they left, too."

control supervise or manage
upset disturbed

The boy said, "Yes. Everything in nature **interacts** with one another. Plant flowers and butterfly bushes, and the bees and butterflies will come back. Then birds will come back, too."

So the villagers **planted** new butterfly bushes and added more flowers.

Soon, their garden was the most beautiful garden in the world once again.

interacts connects
planted put in the ground

When the visitor returned to the village, he found the villagers **disguised** as birds, bees, and butterflies running toward him to **prevent** his entry. The visitor ran away as fast as he could, and the villagers laughed as he ran.

Once he was gone, the boy who lived outside the village turned to them and smiled. He said, "Ah, what does a visitor know?" ❖

disguised wearing costumes
prevent stop

▶ **Before You Continue**

1. **Confirm Prediction** How did the villagers get their garden back to the way it was? Was your prediction correct?

2. **Compare/Contrast** What do the villagers think about the visitor's advice at the beginning and end of the story? What do they learn?

Think and Respond

Key Words	
amount	increase
balance	interact
behavior	react
control	scarce
decrease	supply

Talk About It

1. What is the funniest part of this **humorous story**? Tell your opinion.

To me, the funniest part _____ .

2. What do you think the visitor might say if he saw the garden at the end of the story? Pretend to be the visitor and give your opinion about the garden.

"I think this garden _____ ."

3. What do the villagers learn from the boy? What do they do as a result?

The villagers learned that _____ .
As a result, they _____ .

Write About It

Imagine that your own community gets out of **balance**. What could make it get out of balance? How would people **react**? Write two sentences. Use at least one **Key Word**.

When a lot of _____ , things get _____ .
People _____ .

Compare and Contrast

Make a Venn diagram for "It's All in the Balance." Use the pictures and the text to compare and contrast the visitor with the boy.

Venn Diagram

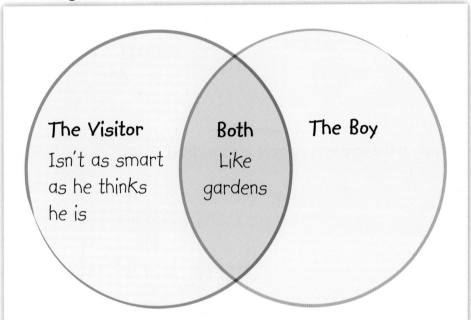

The Visitor
Isn't as smart as he thinks he is

Both
Like gardens

The Boy

Use your diagram to tell a partner how the visitor and the boy are alike and how they are different. Use the sentence frames and **Key Words**. Record your comparison.

They are alike because _____ .
The visitor _____ , but the boy _____ .

Fluency

Practice reading with expression. Rate your reading.

Talk Together

What happens to the garden when nature loses its **balance**? Describe the garden before and after. Use **Key Words**.

101

Syllables

In a dictionary, a word may be divided into **syllables**, or word parts.

Look at this example of a dictionary entry. How many syllables does **supply** have?

This part shows how to divide the word into syllables.

sup•ply *noun* A supply is the amount you have of something.

Try It Together

Use the dictionary entries to answer the questions.

in•ter•act *verb* To interact means to act together.
scarce *adjective* When something is scarce, it is hard to find or get.

1. **How many syllables does interact have?**

   A one

   B two

   C three

   D four

2. **Scarce is a one-syllable word. How can you tell?**

   A It is hard to say.

   B It is not divided.

   C It is an adjective.

   D It has only six letters.

Animals, More or Less

by Mike Thaler ✳ illustrated by Jared Lee

What did the sick worm have?

Hint:
We get sick when we **come into contact with** germs.

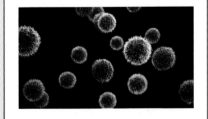

a worm germ

come into contact with touch

▶ **Before You Continue**
1. **Identify** What kind of playful language does this riddle use?
2. **Apply** Using one or two words from this page in a playful way, make up a riddle of your own. Try it on a partner.

What can too many **hares** in the air cause?

hare pollution

Hint:

Too many poisons in the air can cause air pollution.

hare an animal very similar to a rabbit

What does one lonely buffalo do when it sees other buffalos?

It tries to be herd.

Hint:
A **herd** of animals is noisy. It can be **heard** as it runs across the plains.

herd group
heard listened to

▶ **Before You Continue**
1. **Identify** What kinds of playful language do the riddles on pages 104–105 use?
2. **Apply** Find words on the page that have multiple meanings. Use one or two of them to make up your own riddle.

What happens when too few acorns fall from the trees?

The squirrels go nuts!

Hint: Acorns are nuts that squirrels like to eat.

go nuts act in a strange or silly way

What happens when there are too many frogs on a baseball team?

Hint:
Frogs eat **flies**. But in baseball, flies are balls hit high into the air.

They catch all the flies. ❖

flies insects; high balls in baseball that when caught count as outs

▶ **Before You Continue**
1. **Identify** What kind of playful language do the riddles on pages 106–107 use?
2. **Apply** Find the multiple meaning words in the riddles. Then use them to make up your own riddles. Share them with the class.

107

Respond and Extend

Key Words

amount	increase
balance	interact
behavior	react
control	scarce
decrease	supply

Compare Genres

"It's All in the Balance" is a humorous story. "Animals, More or Less" has riddles. How are a humorous story and a riddle alike? How are the two genres different? Complete the checklist chart with a partner.

Checklist Chart

Think about each description.

	Humorous Story	Riddle
funny	✔	✔
usually long		
short		
playful language		
paragraphs		
questions and answers		

Write check marks to show whether the words describe a humorous story, a riddle, or both.

Talk Together

What happens when nature loses its **balance**? Think about the story and the riddles. Use **Key Words** to talk about your ideas.

Kinds of Sentences

There are four kinds of sentences.

Grammar Rules Kinds of Sentences

• Use a **statement** to tell something.	The visitor is in the village**.**
• Use an **exclamation point** to show strong feeling.	The garden looks terrible**!**
• Use a **command** to tell someone to do something.	Dig out the butterfly bushes**.** Stop those caterpillars**!**
• Use a **question** to ask something. Some **question words** are: *Is, Are, Do, Does, Who, What, When, Where.* Some answers have **contractions**.	**Is** the boy foolish**?** No, he **isn't**. **What** is that**? It's** a wheelbarrow. **Do** you like the garden**?** Yes, I do.

Read Sentences

Read this passage about the story. How many kinds of sentences can you find? Tell a partner about the sentences.

The villagers remove the butterfly bushes from the garden. Now the garden looks terrible! What will the villagers do?

Write Sentences

Write three questions about a garden. Your partner writes answers. Are there contractions in any of the answers?

109

PART 2

Language Focus

Language Frames

- Show me _____ .
- Point to _____ .
- Watch out!
- Be careful!

Give and Carry Out Commands

Listen to Rico's song. Then pretend you are somewhere outside, such as by a pond or in a forest. Use **Language Frames** with a partner to give and carry out commands.

Watch Out!

Song

Watch out! Keep away from the water.
Watch out! Keep away from the water.
Point to the clams, but don't get close.
Watch out or you'll slip in the water.

A crab, and a snail, and a
   starfish, too,
All of them live in the
   tidepool zoo.
Show me the clams and
   anemones.
But do not touch them.
   Be careful, please!

Tune: "Boom! Boom! Ain't It Great!"

crab

clam

sea snail

sea anemone

starfish

Key Words
drought
ecosystem
food chain
level
river

🔊 Key Words

Look at these pictures of two **ecosystems**. Use **Key Words** and other words to talk about each place.

◀ Bears catch fish in a **river**. If the bears eat too many fish, it will affect the **food chain**.

◀ In a **drought**, the water **level** falls. Elephants have less water to drink.

Talk Together

Imagine that you and your partner are by the water in the pictures. Use **Language Frames** from page 110 to give and carry out commands. Then use **Key Words** to discuss how an ecosystem can lose its balance.

Cause and Effect

A **cause** makes something happen. An **effect** is what happens. When you identify causes and effects, what you read, see, or hear becomes clearer.

Look at these pictures. Read the captions.

▲ **Water gets trapped in rocks.**

▲ **A tide pool forms.**

Map and Talk

You can use a cause-and-effect diagram to show what happens and why it happens. Here's how you make one.

A cause goes in the first box. The effect goes in the second box.

Cause-and-Effect Diagram

Cause | Effect

Tell why something happens here.

Ocean water gets trapped in rocks.

A tide pool forms.

Tell what happens here.

Talk Together

Look back at page 111. Find a cause and an effect. Make a diagram to show what happens, and why. Explain your diagram to a partner.

More Key Words

Use these words to talk about "When the Wolves Returned" and "Megafish Man."

competition
noun

A **competition** is a contest or struggle between two or more people or animals.

nature
noun

Nature means things like rivers, trees, and animals. She likes to study **nature**.

negative
adjective

Something that is **negative** is bad. Screaming at someone is a **negative** action.

positive
adjective

Something that is **positive** is good for you. Exercise is a **positive** activity.

resources
noun

Resources are things that you can use. A library has many **resources**.

Talk Together

Work with a partner. Make a Word Web of examples for each **Key Word**.

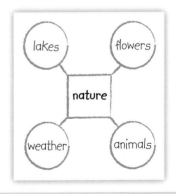

113

Learn to Ask Questions

Do you want to know more about this picture? If so, **ask** yourself **questions**. To figure out the answers, take a closer look at the picture, or think about what you know about **ecosystems**.

◀ **This photo shows a tiny ecosystem.**

As you read, **ask questions**. You can find the answers to some questions in your head. Think to come up with answers. This will help you understand the text better.

How to Ask Questions

❓	**1.** Ask a question.	I wonder: _____ ?
☁	**2.** Think about your experiences and what you know. Think about what the author is trying to tell you.	I know _____ . The author _____ .
☁	**3.** Think about the answer. Read on and ask more questions.	So _____ . Now I wonder: _____ ?

Language Frames

?   I wonder:
     _____ ?

   I know _____ .
   The author
     _____ .

   So _____ .
   Now I wonder:
     _____ ?

Talk Together

Read Rico's report with a partner. Read the sample questions. Then use **Language Frames** to ask and answer questions to check your understanding. Tell a partner about them.

Report

What Makes an Ecosystem?

by Rico Borelli

An **ecosystem** is made up of living and nonliving things. Each thing interacts with everything else in the system. An ecosystem needs **resources** . These resources include soil, sunlight, and water. Dead plants and other wastes play a **positive** part, too. They put nutrients into the soil.

Plants take nutrients from the soil. Plant-eaters eat the plants. Predators eat the plant-eaters. This **food chain** keeps the ecosystem in balance. That means there is never too much or too little of any one thing.

Prey and predators eat to stay alive. So there is always **competition** for food in an ecosystem. Sometimes one kind of animal eats too many of another kind. This will have a **negative** effect. It throws the system out of balance.

There are many different ecosystems in **nature** . Some are large, like forests and deserts. Others are as small as a crack in a tree. But every one of them is part of the largest ecosystem of all: planet Earth.

Sample Questions

"I wonder: What are the resources?

I know that water, sun, and soil are important. The author probably means those resources.

So I learn that I'm right. Now I wonder: What do dead plants do in an ecosystem?"

◀ = A good place to ask a question

Vowel Sounds and Spellings: *oo*

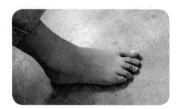

foot

book

Listen and Learn

Listen to each sentence. Choose the word that best completes the sentence.

1. We needed some _____ to make a fire.

wedge   group   wood

2. Please hang your coat on the _____.

hand   truck   hook

3. I need to read this _____ by Monday.

book   born   bank

4. The _____ made us a nice dinner.

chute   cook   core

Listen and read. Find the words with the vowel sound you hear in the word *book* spelled *oo*.

Over to You

The Hike

Mateo and Juan went on a hike through the sandy, rocky hills.

"I'm too hot," groaned Mateo. "I don't think I can walk much farther."

"Have some water," Juan suggested. "Some hikers have a negative experience because they aren't prepared."

The boys continued walking. "Point to the river on the map," said Mateo.

Juan took out the map and pointed to the river. "There was a drought," said Juan. "The water level is very low."

Suddenly Mateo shouted, "Watch out for that snake!"

The snake slipped into the rocks. "It's good that you saw it," said Juan.

The boys climbed to the top of a hill. The river was below. Mateo raced down the hill.

"Be careful!" yelled Juan, but it was too late. Mateo slipped in the mud and fell over.

Juan stood over him. "Would you say this was a negative hiking experience?"

Mateo shook his head. "Well, at least I'm cool now, so I guess it must be positive!"

Work with a partner.

Choose two words from the story with the vowel sound you hear in *book*. Take turns with your partner making up sentences using the words.

◄ Practice reading words with the vowel sound you hear in *book* by reading "The Hike" with a partner.

Read a Science Article

Genre

A **science article** is nonfiction. It can explain why certain things happen in nature.

Text Feature

A **time line** shows a sequence of important events. It tells about each event and when it happened.

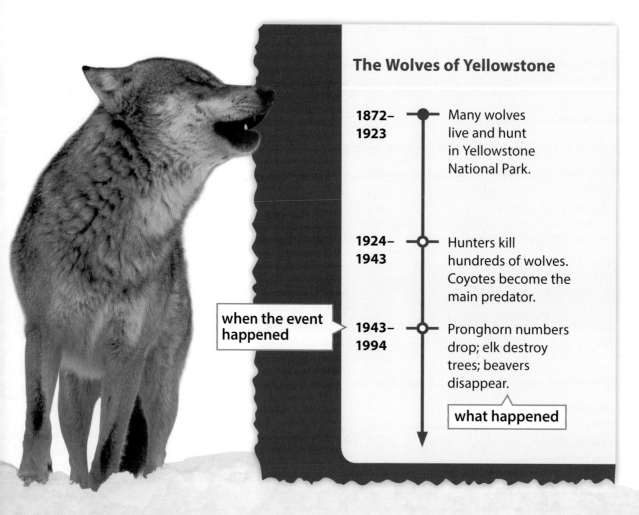

The Wolves of Yellowstone

1872–1923	Many wolves live and hunt in Yellowstone National Park.
1924–1943	Hunters kill hundreds of wolves. Coyotes become the main predator.
1943–1994	Pronghorn numbers drop; elk destroy trees; beavers disappear.

when the event happened

what happened

WHEN THE WOLVES RETURNED

adapted from a book by **DOROTHY HINSHAW PATENT**

THE FIRST NATIONAL PARK

Where would you go to see some of Earth's natural wonders? You might go to a place called Yellowstone. In Yellowstone, **geysers shoot steam** high into the air and waterfalls flow into colorful canyons. All kinds of wildlife roam the land. This special place became the world's first **national park** in 1872.

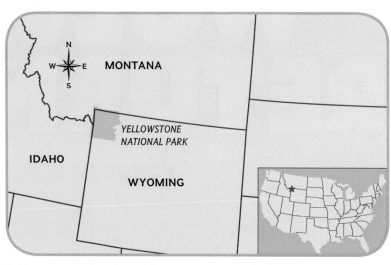

Yellowstone National Park is **primarily** in Wyoming, USA.

▲ Yellowstone has many waterfalls.

▲ Steam rises from a geyser.

geysers shoot steam hot water comes up from under the ground
national park protected area of land
primarily mainly

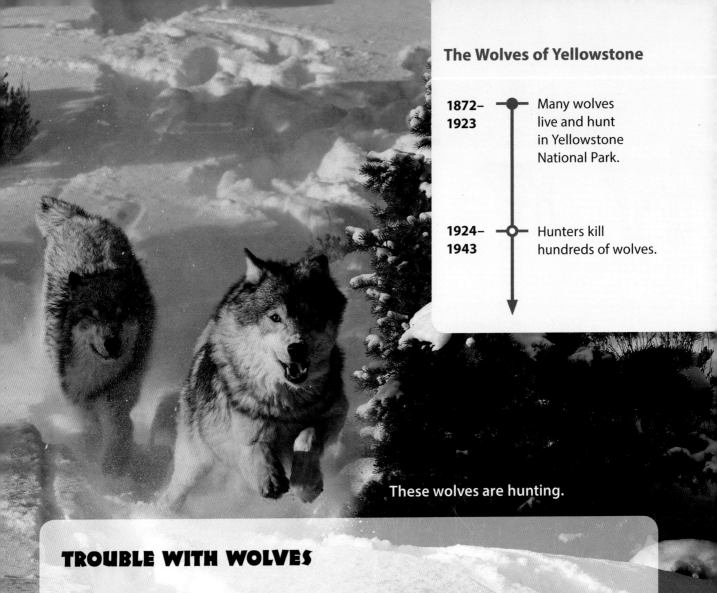

The Wolves of Yellowstone

1872–1923 — Many wolves live and hunt in Yellowstone National Park.

1924–1943 — Hunters kill hundreds of wolves.

These wolves are hunting.

TROUBLE WITH WOLVES

The purpose for making Yellowstone a national park was to protect its natural wonders for visitors. People enjoyed seeing animals, like elk and deer, in the park too. But wolves **fed on** them. So, hunters were paid to kill the wolves. **Park officials** did not understand that killing the wolves would **throw nature out of balance**.

fed on killed and ate
Park officials People in charge of Yellowstone
throw nature out of balance change the way animals usually live and die

▶ **Before You Continue**

1. **Cause/Effect** Why did the United States make Yellowstone a national park?
2. **Explain** Tell why wolves were a problem when Yellowstone first opened. Use your own words.

▲ The wolves disappeared. More and more elk filled the park.

YELLOWSTONE WITHOUT WOLVES

By 1926 the wolves were all gone. Without wolves to hunt them, the number of elk increased. To control the elk population, **rangers** trapped them and sent them to other parks. Rangers also had to shoot and kill the elk to keep their numbers down.

▲ fox

rangers park workers

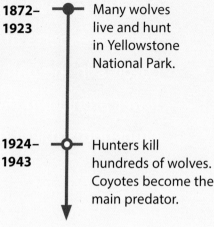

1872–1923	●	Many wolves live and hunt in Yellowstone National Park.
1924–1943	○	Hunters kill hundreds of wolves. Coyotes become the main predator.

▲ coyote

main predator top killer
calves babies

Coyotes also increased in number. Without wolves at the top of the **food chain**, they became Yellowstone's **main predator**. Coyotes eat everything from elk **calves** to insects. But mostly they eat small animals like ground squirrels. So coyotes made it harder for other small predators, like foxes, to find food.

▶ **Before You Continue**

1. **Cause/Effect** The wolves disappeared. What were the effects of that event on the **food chain**?

2. **Ask Questions** What questions might visitors have asked the park rangers in 1926?

PRONGHORNS IN DANGER

Coyotes in Yellowstone also fed on newborn **pronghorns**. They became experts at finding pronghorn **fawns**. With so many coyotes in the park, pronghorn numbers dropped. Every year, fewer pronghorn fawns survived. Park managers worried that pronghorns might disappear completely.

▲ **pronghorn fawns**

pronghorns animals that look like deer
fawns babies

NEW PLANTS DON'T GROW

Even the trees and shrubs **suffered** because the wolves were gone. The elk ate **young shoots** and bark. Young trees and shrubs could not grow fast enough to replace the old ones that died. Soon, the birds that **nested** in the trees and bushes became **rare**.

The Wolves of Yellowstone

1872–1923 — Many wolves live and hunt in Yellowstone National Park.

1924–1943 — Hunters kill hundreds of wolves. Coyotes become the main predator.

1943–1994 — Pronghorn numbers drop; elk destroy trees.

An elk eats young shoots.

suffered experienced **negative** effects
young shoots new plants
nested made their homes
rare fewer in number

▶ Before You Continue

1. **Ask Questions** Ask a question about the pronghorns or elks in Yellowstone. Tell a partner how you plan to find the answer.
2. **Sequence** What happened that led to some birds becoming rare in Yellowstone? Tell the events in order. Use your own words.

A beaver builds a dam.

BEAVERS DISAPPEAR

Beavers use their teeth to cut down trees. They **store** the trees to eat during the winter. They also use the trees to build **dams**. Beaver dams create ponds that provide homes for ducks and other animals.

Without trees, the beavers could not survive. They were almost gone from part of the park by the 1950s.

store save
dams walls that hold back water

A SOLUTION

Many of the problems in the park began soon after the wolves were **eliminated**. Scientists predicted that bringing wolves back would help. Wolves could control the numbers of coyotes and elk. This would **allow** plants and other animals to live and grow.

squirrel

The Wolves of Yellowstone

1872–1923	Many wolves live and hunt in Yellowstone National Park.
1924–1943	Hunters kill hundreds of wolves. Coyotes become the main predator.
1943–1994	Pronghorn numbers drop; elk destroy trees; beavers disappear.

eliminated killed
allow make it possible for

▶ Before You Continue

1. **Cause/Effect** When the beavers left, other animals in Yellowstone lost their homes. Why?
2. **Summarize** What have you learned so far about wolves? How do they affect the balance of **nature** in Yellowstone?

THE WOLVES RETURN

Wolves from Canada were brought to Yellowstone in 1995 and 1996. Seven groups of wolves were set free in the park. Each **pack** lived in a wide area called a territory. It didn't take long for the wolves to **feel at home**. There were a lot of animals, especially elk, for them to hunt.

Year by year, the number of wolves in Yellowstone grew. When a pack became too big, it broke into smaller packs. These groups slowly filled the park. Now, about twelve wolf packs live in Yellowstone. There are usually around 150 wolves in the park.

▲ **young wolves**

pack group of wolves
feel at home enjoy living in Yellowstone

The Wolves of Yellowstone

1872–1923 Many wolves live and hunt in Yellowstone National Park.

1924–1943 Hunters kill hundreds of wolves. Coyotes become the main predator.

1943–1994 Pronghorn numbers drop; elk destroy trees; beavers disappear.

1995–1996 Wolves return to Yellowstone.

▶ Before You Continue

1. **Use Text Features/Make Inferences** What probably helped the wolf packs from Canada grow in Yellowstone?

2. **Evaluate** Was it a good idea to return wolves to Yellowstone? Use facts from the text to support your answer.

NATURE'S BALANCE RETURNS

Wolves saw the coyotes as **competition**. They killed coyotes or chased them out of their territories. Now, with fewer coyotes hunting them, pronghorn and other animals survive more easily. Foxes, owls, and other animals also **benefit**. There are fewer coyotes to **compete** with them for the same food.

Without wolves, elk **lingered along the streams** in the park. They ate young trees before they had a chance to grow. Now the elk must keep moving. This makes it harder for wolves to find them. Because the elk are moving, trees can grow again.

▲ Elk keep moving. They want to stay away from wolves.

benefit do better
compete fight
lingered along the streams stayed near the small **rivers**

The Wolves of Yellowstone

1872–1923	●	Many wolves live and hunt in Yellowstone National Park.
1924–1943	○	Hunters kill hundreds of wolves. Coyotes become the main predator.
1943–1994	○	Pronghorn numbers drop; elk destroy trees; beavers disappear.
1995–1996	○	Wolves return to Yellowstone.

▶ **Before You Continue**

1. **Cause/Effect** How do wolves help pronghorn survive?
2. **Details** What do elk do to stay safe from wolves?

▲ beaver

▲ owl

BEAVERS COME BACK

The animals that need the trees are also coming back. For example, in 1996 only one **beaver colony** lived in the northern part of the park. By 2003, there were nine. Scientists hope that birds that hunt from trees, like owls, will also **become more common**.

beaver colony group of beavers
become more common increase in number

A BALANCED ECOSYSTEM

Returning the wolf is helping to make Yellowstone **whole again**. Scientists hope that as the years go by, even more plants and animals will come back. Today, Yellowstone is becoming a healthy system again, thanks to the wolves' return. ❖

The Wolves of Yellowstone

1872– 1923	Many wolves live and hunt in Yellowstone National Park.
1924– 1943	Hunters kill hundreds of wolves. Coyotes become the main predator.
1943– 1994	Pronghorn numbers drop; elk destroy trees; beavers disappear.
1995– 1996	Wolves return to Yellowstone.
1997– today	Wolf packs continue to increase. Nature's balance improves.

whole again a balanced **ecosystem**

▶ **Before You Continue**

1. **Details** Name two animals that need the trees in Yellowstone.
2. **Author's Purpose** What is this article about? Why did the author write it?

Key Words	
competition	nature
drought	negative
ecosystem	positive
food chain	resources
level	river

Talk About It

1. What did you learn about animals in this **science article**? Give two facts.

   I learned _____ . I also learned _____ .

2. Imagine you work at Yellowstone Park. What might a visitor ask you about the history of wolves in the park? **Ask and answer** the question.

   Why were wolves _____ ? Wolves were _____ because _____ !

3. Wolves, coyotes, and elk are part of the **food chain** in Yellowstone. Explain how this part of the chain works. What does each animal eat?

   Wolves eat _____ , and coyotes eat _____ . Elk eat _____ .

Write About It

In folk tales and other stories, wolves are often **negative** characters. Why do you think this is so? Do you think it is fair? Write two or three sentences to explain your thoughts. Use **Key Words**.

Wolves are often negative characters because _____ .
I think/do not think this is fair because _____ .

Cause and Effect

Complete a cause-and-effect diagram for "When the Wolves Returned."

Cause-and-Effect Diagram

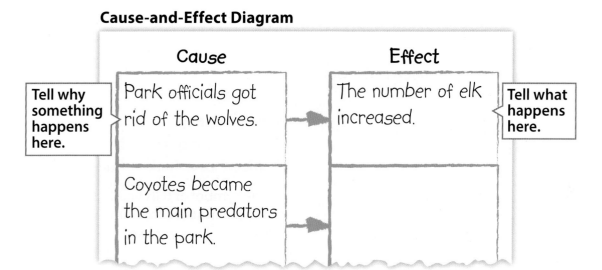

Tell why something happens here.

Cause	Effect
Park officials got rid of the wolves.	The number of elk increased.
Coyotes became the main predators in the park.	

Tell what happens here.

Now use your diagram to retell the information in the article to a partner. Tell each cause. Then use the sentence frame to tell the effect. Use as many **Key Words** as you can. Record your retelling.

This happened, so _____ .

Fluency

Practice phrasing as you read. Rate your reading.

Talk Together

How did **nature** lose its balance in Yellowstone? Summarize the events for a partner. Use **Key Words**.

Pronunciation

Suppose you are unsure about how to say a word. You can use a dictionary to determine the **pronunciation**.

Look at these examples from a dictionary.

This part tells you how to pronounce the word.

na•ture /ˈneɪtʃɚ/ *noun* Nature means things like rivers, trees, and animals.

Pronunciation Key:
hat/**hæt**/ got/**gɒt**/ father/ˈfɑðɚ/
box/ˈbɑks/ cake/keɪk/ fruit/ˈfɹut/

The symbol eɪ tells you to say the **a** in **nature** the same way you say the **a** in **cake**.

Try It Together

Use the dictionary entries to complete the items. For the second item, look at the pronunciation key above, too.

com•pe•ti•tion /ˌkɑmpəˈtɪʃən/ *noun* A competition is a contest or struggle between two or more people or animals.
pos•i•tive /ˈpɒzətɪv/ *adjective* Something that is positive is good for you.

1. **When you say competition, you stress the _____ part.**
   - **A** first
   - **B** second
   - **C** third
   - **D** fourth

2. **You say the o in positive the same way you say the a in _____ .**
   - **A** hat
   - **B** cake
   - **C** wash
   - **D** nature

NATIONAL
GEOGRAPHIC
EXCLUSIVE

Making Connections Now read about an explorer who works to keep a **river ecosystem** healthy.

Genre A **human interest feature** gives facts about someone. It tells what the person does and cares about.

Megafish Man

by **Michael Sandler**

⚠ **Zeb Hogan** [*left*] **with a river stingray**

The telephone rang. Zeb Hogan got the news. A fisherman in Cambodia had caught a giant **river** stingray. Soon, Zeb was **headed** there by plane. "These catches are so **rare**, I don't want to miss out on any of them," he says.

Megafish Man a man interested in very large fish
headed on his way
rare special; unusual

▶ **Before You Continue**

1. **Ask Questions** What questions do you have about Mr. Hogan? How will your questions help you as you read on?

2. **Use Text Features** What helps you figure out what a stingray is?

Monsters of the Mekong

Zeb is an **aquatic ecologist**. He is always searching for megafish. Megafish are aquatic monsters that grow to at least 6.5 feet (2 meters) or 220 pounds (100 kg). He studies the megafish that live in the Mekong **River** in Southeast Asia. Many megafish live in this river and the smaller rivers that **flow** into it.

Megafish

▲ giant skeetfish   ▲ giant stingray   ▲ giant carp

Mekong the Mekong **River**
aquatic ecologist scientist who studies water animals and how they live
flow go

People in Cambodia fish in the Mekong River.

Why is Zeb so interested in megafish? By studying megafish, we can learn a lot about the health of an aquatic **ecosystem**. "If you still have these giant fish **species** in the **river**, it's a good **indication** that the river is healthy," he says.

For centuries, the Mekong's fish of all sizes **thrived** in clean water. There were so many fish, Cambodians often said, "Where there is water, there are fish."

species types
indication sign
thrived lived well

▶ **Before You Continue**

1. **Make Inferences** What details in the text help the reader understand whether these "aquatic monsters" are helpful or harmful?
2. **Clarify** What do **levels**, or numbers, of megafish tell about the health of a **river**?

A River in Trouble

Today, however, fewer and fewer big fish are found in the Mekong. To Zeb, it's a warning. Something is **out of balance**.

Overfishing is one cause of fewer fish. **Pollution** is another. Soon there may be fewer smaller fish, too. This will hurt people who need the fish for food.

A woman sells fish at the market. ▶

▼ **People weigh a giant catfish. There are few left.**

out of balance not right
Overfishing People taking too many fish from the **river**
Pollution Dirty water

▲ Zeb Hogan (*left, with cap*) looks at a stingray. It was caught by a fisherman.

Zeb wants to make Mekong waters healthy again. In Cambodia, he **set up a program**. When fishermen catch megafish, they give them to Zeb. He lets the fish go and **tracks their movements**.

This program **benefits** both the fishermen and the fish. It also helps Zeb learn how to better protect megafish and the **river** so many people and animals **depend on**. ❖

set up a program made a plan
tracks their movements watches where they go
benefits is good for; helps
depend on need to help them live

▶ **Before You Continue**
1. **Cause/Effect** Why are fewer big fish found in the Mekong **River** today than in the past?
2. **Goal/Outcome** What is Mr. Hogan's goal? What has he done to try to reach that goal?

Key Words

competition	nature
drought	negative
ecosystem	positive
food chain	resources
level	river

Compare Ecosystems

List five facts about the **ecosystem** in "When the Wolves Returned" or "Megafish Man." Look back at the selection to locate facts about:

- where the ecosystem is

- what the natural features are

- what animals live in the ecosystem

- why it was or is out of balance

Find a partner who wrote about the other ecosystem. Use your lists to create a comparison chart.

Comparison Chart

Yellowstone Park	Mekong River
Is in the United States	Is in Cambodia

Now discuss your chart. What is different about the two ecosystems? What is the same?

Talk Together

What happens when ecosystems lose their balance? Think about the article and the feature. Use **Key Words** in your discussion.

Compound Sentences

You can use the words *and, but,* or *or* to put two sentences together. When you make a **compound sentence**, put a comma (**,**) before *and, but,* or *or*.

Grammar Rules Compound Sentences	
• Use **and** to join two ideas that are alike.	The wolves hunt coyotes**, and** the coyotes hunt squirrels.
• Use **but** to join two ideas that show a difference.	The fox is little**, but** the bear is big.
• Use **or** to show a choice between two ideas.	We can visit a national park**, or** we can go to the beach.

Read Compound Sentences

Read these sentences about Yellowstone Park. Identify two compound sentences. Point to the word in each sentence that joins the ideas.

> Yellowstone is a special place. Geysers shoot steam up into the air, and waterfalls spill over rocks. You can look at these natural wonders, or you can watch the animals.

Write Compound Sentences

Look at the picture of the beaver on page 126. Write a compound sentence to go with the picture. Read your sentence to a partner.

Write as a Recorder

Write a Summary 🖉

Write a summary of something you read about the balance of nature. Add your summary to a class nature magazine.

Study a Model

In a summary, you present the most important ideas about something you have read or learned in another way.

The title gives the focus of the summary.

Without Wolves
by Jessie Landon

Officials at Yellowstone Park once thought wolves were killing too many of the other animals. So they paid hunters to kill all the wolves.

Park officials quickly learned that this was a mistake. Without the wolves, animals like elk and coyotes grew in number. Soon they were out of control.

The elk destroyed trees and shrubs. As a result, many birds and beavers could not survive. Meanwhile, the coyotes ate food that smaller animals needed to live.

Scientists finally figured out what to do. They brought wolves back to Yellowstone, and the ecosystem got better.

The summary contains only the most important ideas. All the ideas in the article are about the same topic.

The summary has a beginning, a middle, and an end. The writing is complete.

Prewrite

1. **Choose a Topic** What are the most interesting things you have learned about the balance of nature? Talk with a partner to choose one set of ideas to summarize.

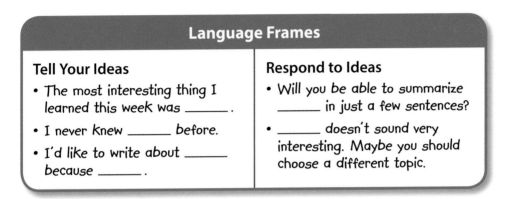

Language Frames

Tell Your Ideas	Respond to Ideas
• The most interesting thing I learned this week was _____ .	• Will you be able to summarize _____ in just a few sentences?
• I never knew _____ before.	• _____ doesn't sound very interesting. Maybe you should choose a different topic.
• I'd like to write about _____ because _____ .	

2. **Gather Information** Reread the information you want to summarize. What are the important ideas? Look at the title, headings, and topic sentences.

3. **Get Organized** Use a chart to help you list the most important ideas. For this article, a cause-and-effect diagram works well.

Cause-and-Effect Diagram

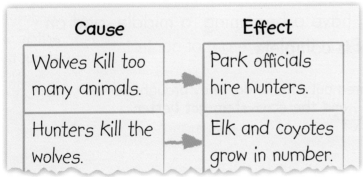

Draft

Use your cause-and-effect diagram to write your draft.

- Include only the most important ideas.
- Make sure all the ideas go together.

Revise

1. **Read, Retell, Respond** Read your summary aloud to a partner. Your partner listens and then retells the important ideas. Next, talk about ways to improve your writing.

Language Frames	
Retell	**Make Suggestions**
• You summarized _____ . • The most important ideas were _____ .	• I think you should take out _____ . It doesn't tell about the topic. • The ending doesn't sound complete. Can you add _____ ?

2. **Make Changes** Think about your draft and your partner's suggestions. Then use revision marks to make your changes.

   • Delete information that doesn't tell about the topic.

   > Without the wolves, animals like elk and coyotes grew in number, and rangers sent many of them to other parks.

   • Does your writing have a beginning, a middle, and an end? Make sure it is complete.

   > Scientists finally figured out what to do. They brought wolves back to Yellowstone. and the ecosystem got better.

Punctuation Tip

✓ Put a comma (,) before **and**, **but**, or **or** in a compound sentence.

Edit and Proofread

Work with a partner to edit and proofread your summary. Punctuate compound sentences correctly. Use revision marks to show your changes.

Present

1. **On Your Own** Make a final copy of your summary. Present it as a short oral report.

Presentation Tips	
If you are the speaker...	**If you are the listener...**
In a summary, every word is important. Be sure to speak slowly and clearly.	Think about whether the summary was clear to you. Did anything seem to be missing?
Repeat any parts of your summary that you say too fast or incorrectly.	Think about what you could learn about summarizing from the example you heard.

2. **With a Group** Illustrate your summary. Then work with your classmates to create a magazine called "Nature Out of Balance." You and your classmates may want to donate the magazine to your school library.

Question

What happens
when nature loses
its balance?

Talk Together

In this unit, you found lots of answers to the **Big Question**. Now,
make a concept map to discuss the **Big Question** with the class.

Concept Map

Animals don't
have enough
food.

things that
happen when
nature loses
its balance

Write a Description ✏️

Select one thing on your concept map that can happen
when nature is not in balance. Write a description of it.

Share Your Ideas

Choose one of these ways to share your ideas about the **Big Question**.

Write It!

Trade Cards

On a slip of paper, write something that could make an ecosystem lose its balance. Trade slips with a partner. Draw an example of your partner's ecosystem. Share and discuss your drawings.

Talk About It!

Share Pictures

Find a picture of a forest, pond, or other ecosystem. Decide whether the place is in balance or out of balance. Explain your picture to the class.

Do It!

Create a Riddle

Create a riddle with a partner. Write about something in nature. Then find another pair of partners. Ask them your riddle. Try to guess theirs!

What did the dog say to the wolves? (Woof! Woof!)

Write It!

Perform a Skit

Write a skit about an ecosystem. The characters are the animals, plants, water, and so on. What do they say about their home? Do they use formal or informal language? Present your skit to the class.

RIVER: It rained. I am full of fresh, clean water!

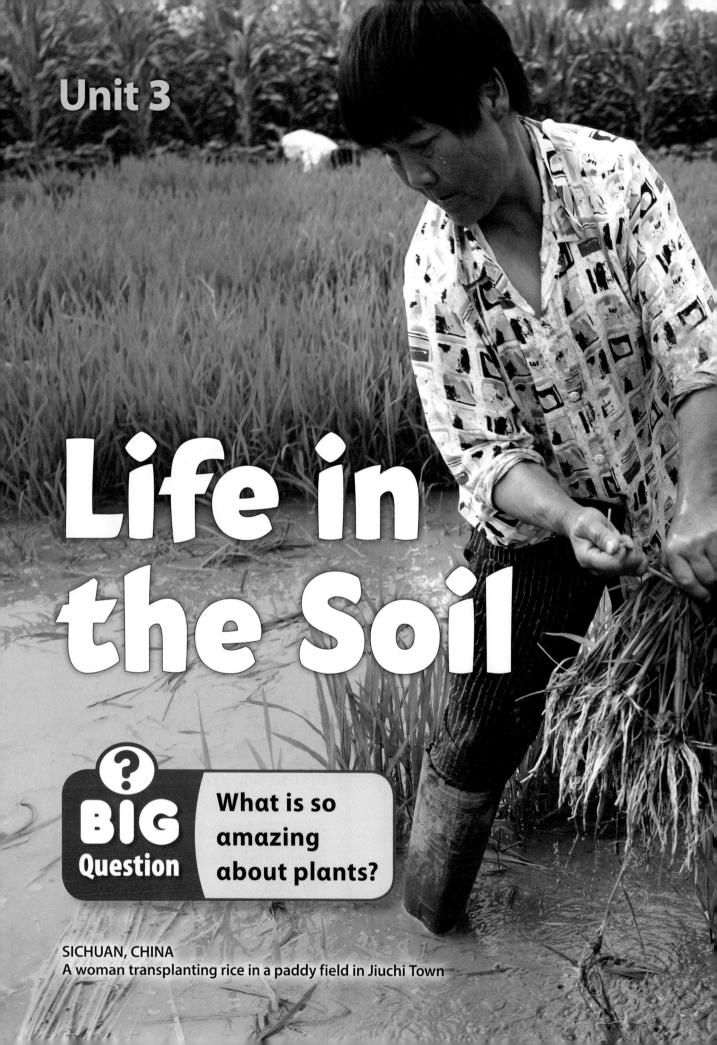

Life in the Soil

BIG Question

What is so amazing about plants?

SICHUAN, CHINA
A woman transplanting rice in a paddy field in Jiuchi Town

Unit at a Glance

▷ **Language Focus**: Give Information, Define and Explain
▷ **Reading Strategy**: Make Inferences
▷ **Phonics Focus**: Review: Two- and Three-Letter Blends; Plurals: *-s, -es, -ies*
▷ **Topic**: Plants

Share What You Know

Do It!

My plant grows without much water.

❶ **Think** of the most amazing plant you know. Draw it.

❷ **Display** all the class drawings. Don't tell which is yours!

❸ **Say** an amazing thing your plant does. Can your class guess which plant is yours?

Give Information

Listen to Marco's song. Then use **Language Frames** to give information about a plant you know.

Song 🔊 ♪

My Big, Strong Plant

A big, strong plant lives in my yard.
Its stem is thick and wide.
Its leaves are nearly two feet long.
I'm glad it lives outside!

Chorus:

My big, strong plant!
It grows against my wall.
It has flowers in the summer
And seed pods in the fall.

Tune: "Oh! Susanna"

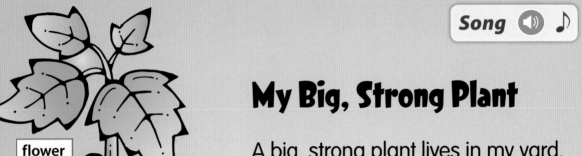

flower

leaf

stem

seed pod

🔊 Key Words

Look at this diagram. Use **Key Words** and other words to talk about the life **cycle** of a pea plant.

Key Words
blossom
cycle
root
seed
soil
sprout

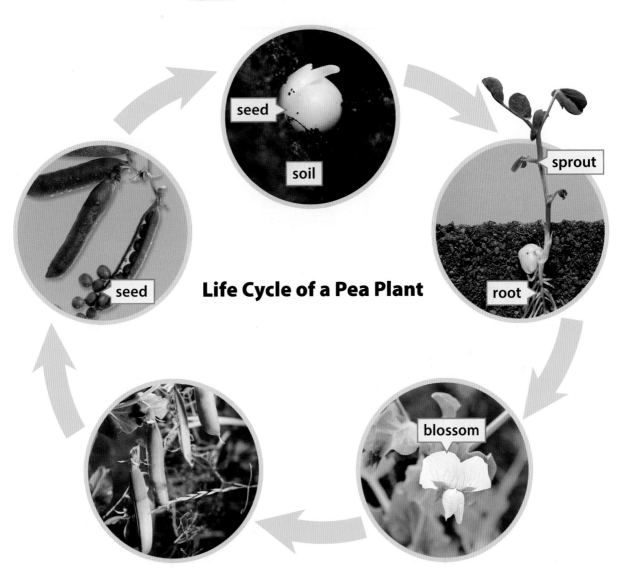

Life Cycle of a Pea Plant

seed

soil

sprout

root

blossom

seed

Talk Together

What is amazing about a pea plant's life cycle? Use **Language Frames** from page 152 and **Key Words** to give information to a partner.

153

Sequence

When things happen in a certain order, they are in **sequence**. When you talk about sequence, you can use:

- time-order words: *first, next, then, finally*
- names of days, months, seasons: *Monday, May, summer*

Look at the pictures of a growing plant.

 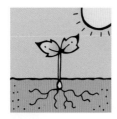  

Map and Talk

You can use a sequence chain to show when events happen. Here's how you make one.

Each event goes in a box in the sequence chain. The first event goes in the first box. The second event goes in the second box, and so on.

Sequence Chain

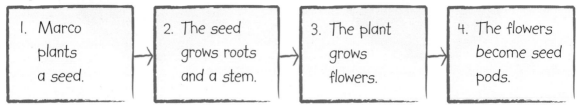

1. Marco plants a seed.
2. The seed grows roots and a stem.
3. The plant grows flowers.
4. The flowers become seed pods.

Talk **Together**

Tell your partner the steps of a plant's life cycle. Your partner makes a sequence chain.

🔊 More Key Words

Use these words to talk about "Hoa's Little Garden" and "Gifts from the Earth."

characteristic
noun

A **characteristic** is how something looks or what something does. A **characteristic** of this plant is white flowers.

conditions
noun

When **conditions** are right, good things happen. Clear skies and wind are good **conditions** for sailing.

depend
verb

To **depend** means to need something or someone for support. A baby **depends** on its mother.

growth
noun

The **growth** of something is how much bigger it gets.

produce
verb

To **produce** means to make something. This factory **produces** cars.

Talk Together

Use a **Key Word** to ask a question. A partner uses a **Key Word** to answer.

What is a characteristic of some plants?

Some plants produce fruit.

Learn to Make Inferences

Look at the picture. The text does not say how Marco and his mom feel. Look at their expressions to figure out, or **make an inference** about, their feelings.

This is for you!

When you read, you have to **make inferences**, too.

How to Make Inferences

👁	**1.** Look for details in the text.	I read _____ .
☁	**2.** Think about what you already know about the details and the topic.	I know _____ .
🧩	**3.** Put your ideas together. What else can you figure out about the details?	And so _____ .

Talk Together

Read Marco's "Gardener's Journal." Read the sample inference. Then use **Language Frames** to make inferences. Tell a partner about them.

Journal

Gardener's Journal

June 15:   I love my big plant! I water it every day. It is in a sunny place, so it has all the right **conditions** to grow.

June 20:   My plant bloomed today! The **blossoms** are bright orange. The color is a **characteristic** of this plant. Tomorrow, I go to Grandma's house for a long visit.

July 10:   I just got back from Grandma's house. My plant looks terrible! I expected a lot of **growth**, but its stem is bent over. I watered it, but I'm so worried.

July 11:   This morning I checked my plant again. It looks fine! The stem is strong and straight. The **soil** is damp and cool.

August 1:   Oh, dear! My plant is in trouble again! It looks like someone has put little holes in its leaves. What can I do? My plant **depends** on me! ◀

August 2:   Dad told me to wash each leaf with dish soap. That sounds crazy!

August 8:   The soap worked! My plant looks great. ◀

September 1: This week my plant **produced** giant pods. I'll plant the **seeds**. Next summer I'll have more big, strong plants!

Sample Inference

"I read that Marco was gone and the plant looks terrible.

I know that some plants need water every day.

And so the plant must need water."

◀ = A good place to make an inference

🔊 Review Two- and Three-Letter Blends

crab

globe

stream

desk

Listen and **Learn**

🔊 Listen to the sounds in the blends. Choose the words with the same sounds.

1.

crack   flip   glad

2.

cross   brick   class

3.

wasp   ask   best

4.

strap   split   screech

🔊 Listen and read. Find the words with beginning and ending blends.

Over to You

What a Plant Needs

The stem of a plant is strong. Its stem is what helps it stand up tall. It has roots that hold it in the ground. Its roots drink water. Its leaves are what take in the sunshine.

Find out what conditions a plant needs to grow. Get some soil, some seeds, and four paper cups. Put soil in two cups and plant some seeds in each one. Give both cups water. Place one cup in the sun and one in a dark closet. Plant seeds in the other two cups, but don't give them any water. Place one of these cups in the sun and the other in the closet. Which seeds sprout? Which seeds grow?

What conditions do plants need to grow? Plants need sunshine. The seeds in the dark do not grow. Plants need water. The seeds with no water do not grow. The seeds that get both sunshine and water sprout and grow tall.

Work with a partner.

Take turns. Find a word from the passage that has a blend and read it aloud. Your partner should find the word and point to it.

◀ Practice reading words with blends by reading "What a Plant Needs" with a partner.

Read a Story

Genre
Realistic fiction is a story that sounds as if it could be true. The characters, plot, and setting all seem real.

Characters
Characters are the people in the story.

Hoa

Mom

Hoa's Little Garden

by Susan Henderson

Hoa loved to walk in the park with her family. She loved the **chirping** birds, the tall trees, and the bright green plants. Most of all, she loved the flowers and their sweet-smelling **blossoms** .

"I wish we could have a garden," Hoa said to her mom.

Hoa's mom smiled. "In our little apartment? Not very likely."

chirping singing

At home, Hoa drew pictures of flowers and plants. She **hung** them all around the apartment. She knew that colorful pictures made the apartment feel **lighter and brighter**.

Hoa's mom picked up one of her drawings. "You're a very talented artist, Hoa," she said.

Hoa **replied**, "If we had real plants and flowers, I wouldn't have to draw them."

"Your name means *flower,*" her mom told her. "Maybe that's why you love flowers so much."

hung put on the wall
lighter and brighter happier and less dark
replied answered

▶ **Before You Continue**
1. **Setting** Where does Hoa live? How do you know?
2. **Make Inferences** What does Hoa like about flowers?

At school, Hoa's class planted bean **seeds** . The plants grew well in the classroom, so Hoa took her bean plant home and set it on a table. But in a few days, her little plant died.

"It doesn't have the right **conditions** to grow," said her mom. "It needs more light."

Hoa wanted a flower garden **badly**, but she knew there was no space for one in her family's apartment.

One day, when Hoa was working on one of her drawings, she looked outside. She saw something she **hadn't noticed** before. The **sun's rays were shining** into a corner of the balcony.

badly very much
hadn't noticed didn't see
sun's rays were shining sunshine was coming
   through

"Mom!" called Hoa. "Come look. The sun is shining on our **balcony**. I can have a garden!"

Her mom laughed. "Well, maybe you can have a *small* garden," she said, "a *very* small garden. You can grow one plant in a pot. But that's it. There is no space for more than one pot."

balcony terrace

Hoa thought about what she should plant. *I love flowers,* she told herself, *but it would be nice to grow something to eat, too.*

Hoa thought about the different types of plants she had learned about at school. *I know! A* **passion fruit** *plant will give us flowers to enjoy* and *fruit to eat.*

passion fruit a tropical fruit with lots of seeds

▶ **Before You Continue**

1. **Confirm Prediction** Was your prediction correct? What else will Hoa need to do to keep her plants growing?
2. **Character** Do Hoa and her mom get along well? How do you know?

167

▶ Predict
Look at the picture. What will
happen to the passion fruit **seeds**?

Hoa's mom got her a pot, a **spade**, and some **soil**. She helped Hoa cut open a passion fruit. Hoa took **a dozen** seeds from inside the fruit and planted them in the dirt.

"Do you think any of these **seeds** will sprout?" she asked her mom.

"I hope so, Hoa," her mom said.

spade small shovel
a dozen twelve

Hoa checked her plant every morning and every night. One night, after weeks of checking, she finally spotted a little **sprout** growing in her pot.

A few weeks later, the sprout had grown into a small **vine**. The vine kept growing and growing until it spilled out of the pot.

"You need a stick for the vine to grow onto," said her mom.

vine creeping plant

Three months later, there was a big purple flower on the vine.

"Mom," Hoa called, "come look! My vine has **produced** a beautiful flower!"

Her mom was very happy for her. "What a wonderful job you did, Hoa." Hoa was **beaming**. She knew the beautiful flower would blossom into a fruit.

beaming smiling brightly

It wasn't long before Hoa's family was enjoying a bowl full of passion fruit. The family's next-door neighbor, Mrs. Nguyen, also had a bowl of passion fruit. Hoa's passion fruit vine had grown so much that it grew onto Mrs. Nguyen's balcony!

Hoa was very happy. Some of the passion fruit were sweet and juicy, and others were **tangy and tart**. But they were all very tasty.

tangy and tart sourish

I'm a great gardener, thought Hoa. She asked her mom for another pot.

"Another pot?" asked her mom. "What do you want to grow now?"

"Chilies," Hoa answered. "Bright red ones!"

Her mom thought for a moment. "Hmmm," she said, "maybe we should ask Mrs. Nguyen if there's enough room on her balcony." ❖

▶ **Before You Continue**

1. **Confirm Prediction** What did you think would happen to the passion fruit **seeds**? Were you surprised?

2. **Point of View** What does Hoa's mom think about Hoa's gardening? How do you know?

Susan Henderson

Susan Henderson likes to grow flowers and basil on her Seattle balcony. She grows blue and red petunias and bright orange marigolds. Her cat, Frankie, likes the pots of grass she grows for him to munch on.

Before she moved to Seattle, the author lived in Australia. She taught many Vietnamese children, who are now grown up and have children of their own. She is still in touch with some of them through e-mail.

The author loves to read. She also enjoys writing stories that she hopes children will love to read, too.

Writing Tip ✏️

Find places in the story where Susan Henderson helps you see and feel what is happening. Then write your own sentences.

Describe the way your favorite plant looks and feels.

Think and Respond

Key Words

blossom	produce
characteristic	root
conditions	seed
cycle	soil
depend	sprout
growth	

Talk About It

1. What seems **realistic** about the story? Give two examples.

> The story is realistic because _____ .

2. Imagine you are Hoa's mom. **Give information** to Hoa about the life **cycle** of a passion fruit plant.

> First, the plant has _____ . Next, _____ . Then, _____ .

3. Think about the passion fruit that Hoa grew. What were some of its **characteristics**?

> All the passion fruit _____ .
> Some passion fruit _____ . Others _____ .

Write About It

Hoa worked with her mom to grow passion fruit. What do you think Hoa learned about the **growth** of a passion fruit plant? Write two sentences. Use **Key Words** to explain your thinking.

> I think Hoa learned that _____ .

Sequence

Make a sequence chain to show what happens in "Hoa's Little Garden." Notice that some of the events in the sequence influence future events.

Sequence Chain

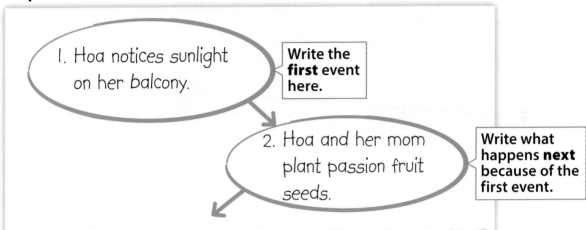

1. Hoa notices sunlight on her balcony.

Write the **first** event here.

2. Hoa and her mom plant passion fruit seeds.

Write what happens **next** because of the first event.

Now use your sequence chain as you retell the story to a partner. Use time-order words and **Key Words**. Record your retelling.

First, _____ .
Next, _____ .
Then, _____ .

Fluency

Practice reading with expression. Rate your reading.

Talk Together

What is amazing about how a passion fruit plant grows? Draw a picture. Use **Key Words** as labels. Share your picture with the class.

Multiple-Meaning Words

Some words have more than one meaning. You can use context, or the words near the word, to figure out the correct meaning.

Roots is a **multiple-meaning word**. Compare these examples.

The plant has long **roots**.
Meaning: the plant part that grows underground

The crowd **roots** for its favorite team.
Meaning: cheers for

Try It Together

Read the sentences. Then answer the questions.

We live in the country. New homes <u>sprout</u> up every year. We sell carrots, bean <u>sprouts</u>, and other vegetables to our new neighbors.

1. What does <u>sprout</u> mean in the second sentence?

　A a new young plant

　B to appear suddenly

　C to grow shoots or buds

　D a plant part you can eat

2. Which word helps you understand the meaning of <u>sprouts</u> in the third sentence?

　A year

　B homes

　C neighbors

　D vegetables

Making Connections Read poems about pineapples and other amazing foods.

Genre A **haiku** is a poem that has three lines. The first line has five syllables. The second line has seven syllables. The last line has five syllables. How many syllables do you count in each poem?

Gifts from the Earth
by Eloise Vivanco

Pineapples

Juicy, delicious,
Under a tropical sun.
Funny, **spiky** hair!

---

spiky sticking up

▶ **Before You Continue**

1. **Make Inferences** Based on the poem, what climate do you think pineapples need to grow in? Explain.
2. **Describe** Name two **characteristics** of pineapples, based on words in the poem.

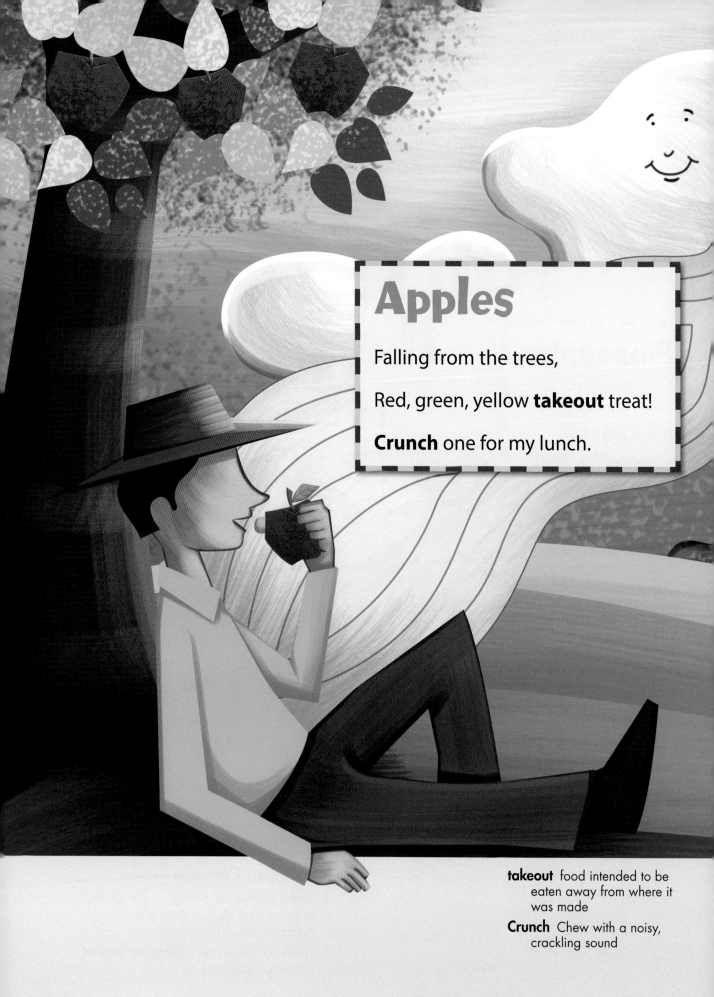

Apples

Falling from the trees,

Red, green, yellow **takeout** treat!

Crunch one for my lunch.

takeout food intended to be eaten away from where it was made

Crunch Chew with a noisy, crackling sound

Five Things You Might Not Know about Apples

- Apples have more **genes** than humans!

- Scientists think apples **originated** in Kazakhstan, but they grow in many countries under many **conditions**.

- There are 3,000 known **varieties** of apples.

- One of the strangest names of a variety of apple is "Winter Banana."

- Apple trees blossom in spring or summer.

Winter banana

genes cells that determine characteristics of a living thing

originated where something began

varieties different types

▶ **Before You Continue**

1. **Make Inferences** Why are apples "takeout food?"

2. **Details** List two facts about apples that you learned by reading the information on this page.

Rice

Green, wet **paddy field,**

Tall grass waving in the **breeze.**

Pass the hot bowl, please! ❖

paddy field a watery field where
    rice is grown
breeze gentle wind

More About Rice

- Rice is a grain, like corn or wheat.
- Rice can be grown in many places, but it needs **mild** conditions.
- In many Asian countries, it is common to eat rice for breakfast.
- Some artists will write your name on a grain of rice!

mild gentle

▸ Before You Continue

1. **Imagery** After reading the poem and looking at the picture, what do you imagine working in a paddy field might be like? What made you imagine it that way?
2. **Details** Name two things you learned about rice from the information on this page.

Compare Genres

A story and a haiku are different forms of writing, or genres. What about the two genres is the same? What about them is different? Work with a partner to complete the Venn diagram.

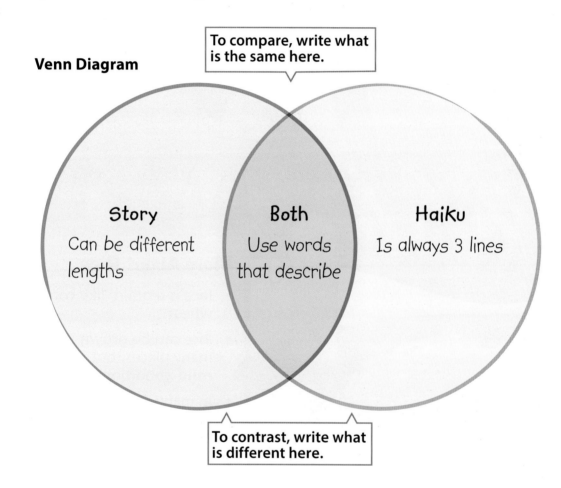

Venn Diagram

To compare, write what is the same here.

Story
Can be different lengths

Both
Use words that describe

Haiku
Is always 3 lines

To contrast, write what is different here.

Talk Together

What is amazing about how a plant grows? Think about the story, the haiku, and the facts about plants. Use **Key Words** to talk about your ideas.

Plural Nouns

A noun names a person, place, thing, or idea. A **singular noun** shows "one." A **plural noun** shows "more than one."

Grammar Rules Plural Nouns

	singular noun	plural noun
• Add -**s** to most nouns to show more than one.	cycle flower	cycle**s** flower**s**
• Add -**es** to nouns that end in **x**, **ch**, **sh**, **ss**, **z**, and sometimes **o**.	bush tomato	bush**es** tomato**es**
• For most nouns that end in **y**, change the **y** to **i** and then add -**es**. For nouns that end with a vowel and **y**, just add -**s**.	berr**i**y̶ famil**i**y̶ boy day	berr**ies** famil**ies** boy**s** day**s**

Read Plural Nouns

Read this passage. What plural nouns can you find?

Hoa loved the chirping birds, the tall trees, and the bright green plants. Most of all, she loved the flowers and their sweet-smelling blossoms.

Write Plural Nouns

What do you see on pages 178–179? Tell your partner what you see. Then write a sentence for your partner. Use a plural noun.

Define and Explain

Listen to Lily and Nico's dialogue. Then use **Language Frames** to define and explain. Talk about places where plants live.

Language Frames

- _____ means _____ .
- For example, _____ .

Dialogue

1.

What does desert mean?

2.

Desert means a place where there is very little rain. Plants in the desert are unusual.

3.

They can store water. For example, this cactus fills its stem with water when rain falls.

4.

They can change to survive. For example, this plant drops its leaves when it is dry.

Key Words

Key Words
city
desert
rainforest
vine
weed

🔊 Key Words

Look at the pictures. Use **Key Words** and other words to talk about ecosystems, or different places where plants live.

city

weed

In cities, plants grow through cracks and in open areas around buildings.

desert

cactus stem

Many plants in deserts have thick stems that can store water.

rainforest

tall tree

vine

broad leaf

In rainforests, broad leaves, tall trees, and climbing vines collect sunlight.

Talk Together

What is amazing about where plants can grow? Talk with a partner. Try to use **Language Frames** from page 184 and **Key Words** to define words and explain your ideas.

Main Idea and Details

When you explain something, start with the most important idea. This is called the **main idea**. Then give **details** to add more information.

Look at the pictures of interesting desert plants. Read the text.

This cactus can store water.

This plant drops leaves to survive.

Map and Talk

You can use a main idea and details diagram to organize information. Here's how you make one.

The main idea goes in the top box. Each detail is listed under the top box.

Main Idea and Details Diagram

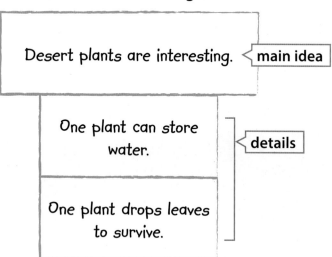

Desert plants are interesting. ⟨ main idea

One plant can store water.
One plant drops leaves to survive.
⟨ details

Talk Together

Look back at page 185. Make a main idea and details diagram with this main idea: **Rainforest plants are unusual.** Tell your partner about your diagram.

More Key Words

Use these words to talk about "A Protected Place" and "Rosie's Reports."

diversity
noun

Diversity means a lot of different people or things. Our school has a great **diversity** of people.

environment
noun

Your **environment** is the kind of place where you live. This is a hot, dry **environment**.

organism
noun

insect

leaf

An **organism** is a living thing. This leaf and insect are both **organisms**.

protect
verb

spine

You **protect** something when you keep it safe. Sharp spines **protect** the plant from animals.

unique
adjective

Unique things are different from other things. The yellow flower is **unique**.

Talk Together

Make a Vocabulary Study Card for each **Key Word**. Write the word on the front.

protect

On the back, write the meaning

to keep safe
A fence protects my garden.

and a sentence. Use the cards to quiz your partner.

187

Learn to Make Inferences

Look at the picture. It does not show the complete plant. Look at the details to figure out, or **make an inference** about, what this plant is like.

When you read, you have to **make inferences**, too.

How to Make Inferences

 1. Look for details in the text.

I read _____.

 2. Think about what you already know about the details and the topic.

I know _____.

 3. Put your ideas together. What else can you figure out about the details?

And so _____.

Talk Together

Read Nico's report, "So Many Plants!" Read the sample inference. Then use **Language Frames** to make inferences. Tell a partner about them.

Report

So Many Plants!
by Nico Lutz

This summer, my family drove to our new home. Along the way, we saw many different **environments**. Our country has such a **diversity** of plants!

In my old home, the ground is covered with sidewalks and streets, but there are still different kinds of plants. People grow plants in pots. Some plants sprout in open areas around buildings.

In another place we saw, there are tall trees all around. Small, leafy plants grow around them. It's a good environment for **organisms** like snails.

Sample Inference

"I read that the ground is covered with sidewalks and streets.

I know that **cities** are like this.

And so they must have lived in a city."

The plants are so different in our new home! The cacti are **unique**. For example, some have round stems. Others have long, thin branches. We have to **protect** ourselves from their sharp spines!

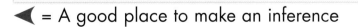

◀ = A good place to make an inference

189

🔊 Plurals -s, -es, -ies

tree + s = trees

dish + es = dishes

puppy + ies = puppies

Listen and Learn

🔊 Listen to each sentence. Choose the correct plural to complete the sentence.

1. I have one **watch**. He has two _____.

watchies   watchs   watches

2. One fluffy **cat** is cute. Two fluffy _____ are even cuter.

cates   cats   caties

3. Tam has one **pony**. Sam has three _____.

ponies   ponys   ponyes

4. Two _____ is better than one **penny**.

pennys   pennies   pennyes

🔊 Listen and read. Find the plural words in the passage.

Amazing Tropical Rainforests

Tropical rainforests are very hot and humid. Rainforests get at least 75 inches of rain each year. Many get even more rain.

There are four layers in a tropical rainforest. The trees in the top two layers are very tall. The top layers get most of the sunlight. The third layer is made up of leaves, branches, and vines. This layer gets much less sunshine. This means that only small plants and trees grow there. The fourth layer is the forest floor. Very little sunlight reaches the forest floor. Hardly any plants grow there. Animals, insects, and birds live in all four layers.

Rainforests help Earth in many ways. For example, they produce 40 percent of the world's oxygen. Rainforests also clean the air of greenhouse gases. They help maintain Earth's water cycle. They also provide foods for people. Finally, half of Earth's animal and plant species live in rainforests. They are truly amazing places.

Work with a partner.

Choose five plural words in the passage and list them. Take turns with your partner to make up new sentences using the words.

◄ Practice reading words with plural endings by reading "Amazing Tropical Rainforests" with a partner.

Read a Science Article

Genre
A science article is **nonfiction**. It gives facts about a topic in nature.

Text Features
Look for **photographs with captions**. They help you understand the text better.

photograph

caption

▲ **An okapi eats leaves.**

A Protected Place

by Elizabeth Sengel

A Special Place

The Okapi Reserve is an amazing place, full of amazing plants. It is in the northeastern corner of Congo and is part of a tropical **rainforest** called the Ituri Forest. The reserve covers 5,200 square miles of land.

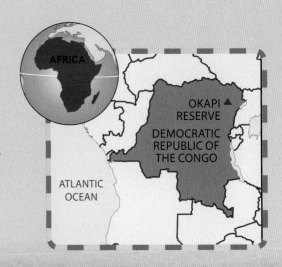

▲ The tops of trees create a cover over the Ituri Forest.

If you flew over the reserve in a plane, all you would see is a thick, green cover. But plant life fills the forest. From top to bottom, it is a tangle of roots, branches, and leaves. The forest **is so dense** that very little sunlight **seeps in**.

is so dense has so many plants
seeps in enters

▶ **Before You Continue**

1. **Main Idea and Details** Give two details about the Okapi Reserve that support the idea that it is an amazing **environment**.

2. **Make Inferences** What would the environment of the Okapi Reserve be like?

A Variety of Plants

One amazing thing about the Okapi Reserve is its **diversity** of plants. There are hundreds of **native species of plants** in the reserve. **Vines** **dangle** from trees. The leaves of giant ferns curve like dinosaur tails. Tall trees reach toward the sky and make a roof with their thick leaves.

▼ A strangler fig grows around another tree in the forest.

giant fern

vines

native species of plants different kinds of plants that grow naturally

dangle hang

▼ An okapi runs through the woods.

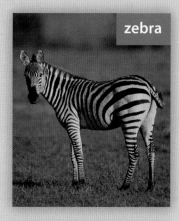

zebra

horse

The Purpose of the Reserve

The Okapi Reserve was created in 1992. The purpose of the reserve is to **protect** the rich **diversity** of plants and animals.

The reserve's name comes from one of those animals—the okapi. This strange-looking animal has the stripes of a zebra and the neck of a horse. But guess what? It's **related to** the giraffe!

giraffe

related to in the same animal family as

▶ **Before You Continue**

1. **Use Text Features** How do the photographs help you understand the text?
2. **Make Inferences** Why was it important to create the reserve?

A Leafy Home

Many different animals, such as elephants,
duikers, and pottos, depend on the forest.
Some of the animals make their homes in trees.

yellow-backed duiker

potto, or tree bear

▼ **An elephant eats plants in the forest.**

Many animals also rely on plants for food. Remember the okapi? It eats the leaves of plants that grow well in the **dim** light of the forest. It has a long tongue that rips the leaves off the branches. The Okapi Reserve has plenty of leaves for okapis to **munch**!

▼ An okapi eats leaves that grow in shady spots.

dim low, weak
munch eat

▶ **Before You Continue**

1. **Make Connections** How does the okapi's long tongue help the animal survive?
2. **Details** Name two ways the plants in the reserve meet the animals' needs.

A Home for Humans

People make their home in the Okapi Reserve, too. **Mbuti Pygmies** have been living in the rainforest for hundreds of years. According to one **botanist**, Mbuti Pygmies are "walking dictionaries of nature." They understand everything about the forest, and they rely on it for food, shelter, and clothing.

▼ **A Mbuti Pygmy** child fishes.

Mbuti Pygmies A group of people native to Africa

botanist scientist who studies plants

Mbuti Pygmies travel from place to place to hunt and fish. They don't just catch **game**, though. They also collect insects, seeds, fruit, and honey to eat. They make nets, arrows, and other **necessities** from forest materials like wood, bark, mud, and leaves.

▼ **Mbuti Pygmies made these huts from forest materials.**

game wild animals to eat
necessities things that
   they need

▶ **Before You Continue**

1. **Make Inferences** Why do you think Pygmies know so much about the **rainforest**?
2. **Details** Name three things that Pygmies do in the forest.

A Brave Botanist

Corneille Ewango is a botanist who works on the reserve. He loves the forest and its plants and animals.

In 1996, something terrible happened. A war **broke out** in Congo. Soldiers **invaded the forest**. They **destroyed** plants and killed animals.

Many of the workers on the reserve ran away, but Ewango wouldn't leave. He knew he had to save the forest. "I was afraid," he says, "but I didn't have a choice."

Soldiers march during the war. ▶

broke out started
invaded the forest came into the forest with force
destroyed ruined

▲ This bridge is important to Ewango. He hid under it once during the war.

Ewango rushed to save what he could. He grabbed computers and buried **data files** in the forest. He packed thousands of **plant samples** in boxes. Friends kept the plants safe.

Ewango hopped on a bicycle and carried other plants into a neighboring country.

Because of Ewango, **unique** and valuable plants were saved. They would continue to grow again after the fighting stopped in 2002.

data files folders with information
plant samples different kinds
    of shrubs, bushes, and trees

▶ **Before You Continue**

1. **Details** Why did Ewango stay in the **rainforest** during the war?
2. **Make Inferences** How do you know that Ewango is a brave person?

The Future of the Reserve

Today, the Okapi Reserve still faces **threats**. Sometimes people destroy animals' homes. They chop down trees. Yet Ewango and other people work every day to solve these problems.

▼ **People sometimes sneak into the Okapi Reserve. They cut down trees.**

threats problems

Ewango believes that Congo needs more scientists to study its forests. He is working hard to **train a new generation of students**.

He wants young people to understand and **protect** the Okapi Reserve and other **rainforests** in Congo. ❖

▼ Ewango wants to train young people. He wants to help protect forests in Congo.

train a new generation of students
teach children about plants

▶ **Before You Continue**

1. **Details** Name two problems that the Okapi Reserve has today.
2. **Paraphrase** What does Ewango believe about Congo? How is he helping?

Key Words

city	protect
desert	rainforest
diversity	unique
environment	vine
organism	weed

Talk About It

1. Give two facts about nature from the **science article**.

   The first fact _____ . The second fact _____ .

2. **Define** the word *reserve* **and explain** the purpose of the Okapi Reserve.

   Reserve means _____ . The purpose of the Okapi Reserve is _____ .

3. How do you think the author of the article feels about the Okapi Reserve **environment**?

   I think the author _____ . I can tell because _____ .

Write About It

The photographs in the science article help you understand the ideas. Write a caption to explain the photograph on page 193. Use at least one sentence and at least one **Key Word**.

This is _____ .

Main Idea and Details

Make a main idea and details diagram for "A Protected Place."

Main Idea and Details Diagram

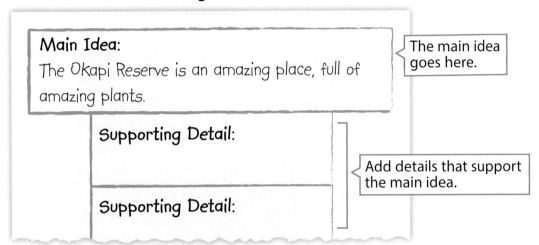

Now use your diagram as you summarize "A Protected Place" for a partner. Use the sentence frames and **Key Words**. Record your summary.

The main idea is _____.
A supporting detail is _____.

Fluency

Practice reading with phrasing. Rate your reading.

Talk Together

Choose a photograph from "A Protected Place." Use **Key Words** to tell a partner what the photograph shows about the Okapi Reserve.

Suffixes

A **suffix** is a word part. A suffix comes at the end of a word. It changes the word's meaning.

Look at this example. How does the word **weed** change?

The suffix -**y** means "full of."

| weed | + | -y | = | weedy |

Weedy means "full of weeds."

Try It Together

Read each item. Choose the correct answer.

1. The suffix <u>-less</u> means "without." What does <u>vineless</u> mean?

    A with vines

    B full of vines

    C without vines

    D the state of vines

2. The suffix <u>-ness</u> means "state of." What does <u>uniqueness</u> mean?

    A in a unique way

    B full of unique things

    C without anything unique

    D the state of being unique

About Rosie's Reports

https://eltngl.com/reachhigherseries

Rosie's Reports

MAIN SCREEN | ABOUT THIS BLOG | PICTURES | REGISTER | SIGN IN

Search All Posts

GO!

About Rosie's Reports

*Rosie Ruf works at the Okapi Reserve. One of her jobs is to take care of several okapis. The okapis are kept in a special **breeding station**. Every day, workers gather fresh leaves for the okapis' food.*

BLOG ARCHIVE
November
September
May
February
January

POSTS BY CATEGORY
okapi
Africa

breeding station place where they can have babies

▶ **Before You Continue**

1. **Make Inferences** How does Rosie probably feel about okapis? Why do you think so?

2. **Predict** What do you think this blog will be about? Explain why you think so.

https://eltngl.com/reachhigherseries

MAIN SCREEN | ABOUT THIS BLOG | PICTURES REGISTER | SIGN IN

Search All Posts

GO!

Category: Okapi | Date: November 8

Collecting Leaves

It is early in the morning. Baya and Apomau are already preparing their **machetes**. They will walk 45 minutes to reach the place where they will cut the leaves for today. In the afternoon, some of the leaves will be fed to the okapis.

◀ **Apomau and Baya have collected and bundled their leaves. It took them less than three hours.**

It is amazing how well they and the other workers know the forest! They are able to find the right amount of leaves every day.

POSTED BY: Rosie

7 COMMENTS   LINKS TO THIS POST

BLOG ARCHIVE
November
September
May
February
January

POSTS BY CATEGORY
okapi
Africa
Okapi Reserve

MOST POPULAR KEYWORDS
protected
rainforest

November						
S	M	T	W	T	F	S
	1	2	3	4	5	6
7	8	9	10	11	12	13
14	15	16	17	18	19	20
21	22	23	24	25	26	27
28	29	30				

‹‹October

machetes large, heavy knives

Preparing Leaves

The workers bring the leaves to a special building. The next step is to prepare 1,536 bundles of leaves! These are the leaves that the okapis will eat in the afternoon and the next morning. ❖

▲ A worker gets ready to wrap a bundle of leaves. The bundle will hang in an okapi's pen.

POSTED BY: Rosie

4 COMMENTS   LINKS TO THIS POST

▶ **Before You Continue**

1. **Make Inferences** Why do you think Baya and Apomau know the **rainforest** so well?
2. **Steps in a Process** List the steps the workers follow to feed the okapis.

Compare Text Features

A science article and a blog post both have captions. What other text features do they both have? What different text features do they have? Work with a partner to complete the comparison chart.

Comparison Chart

"A Protected Place"	"Rosie's Reports"
Feature: captions **Example:** An okapi runs through the woods.	**Feature:** captions **Example:** A worker gets ready to wrap a bundle of leaves.
	Feature: Date line **Example:** Date: November 8

Talk Together

What is amazing about the plants in the Okapi Reserve? Think about the science article and the blog postings. Use **Key Words** to talk about your ideas.

More Plural Nouns

Count nouns are nouns that you can count. They change in different ways to show the plural form.

Noncount nouns are nouns that you cannot count. They have only one form for "one" and "more than one."

Grammar Rules Plural Nouns

Count Nouns		
• Add **-s** or **-es** to make most nouns plural.	tree	▶ tree**s**
	lunch	▶ lunch**es**
• A few nouns use special forms to show the plural.	tooth	▶ teeth
	child	▶ children
Noncount Nouns		
• Use the same form to name "one" and "more than one."	corn	▶ corn
	sunshine	▶ sunshine

Read Plural Nouns

Read these sentences based on "A Protected Place." What plural nouns can you find? Can you identify a noncount noun?

> The forest is a tangle of roots and branches. It is so dense that very little sunlight seeps in.

Write Plural Nouns

Make a list of the things you see on pages 204–205. Compare your list with a partner's.

213

Write Like a Scientist

Write an Article

Write an article that explains what you think is so amazing about plants. Add your article to a class science magazine to share with others in your school.

Study a Model

An article includes facts and details about a topic. Read this article that Mariah wrote about plants.

The **topic sentence** tells the main idea.

Plants Are Everywhere
by Mariah Ruiz

Plants are amazing because they can grow in so many different places. We know that plants grow in soil, but they pop up in other places, too. Did you know that seeds can sprout in tiny cracks on sidewalks? Some daisies, for example, grow big enough to break the pavement!

Other plants, like seaweed, live completely underwater. There are even plants, like mistletoe, that grow on other plants!

So, the next time you're outside, take a look around. You might see a plant or two growing in the most unusual places!

Each **fact** or **detail** supports the main idea. The writing is focused.

The **concluding sentence** connects all the ideas. It makes the writing complete.

Prewrite

1. **Choose a Topic** What topic will you write about in your article? Discuss with a partner to choose the best one.

Language Frames

Tell Your Ideas	Respond to Ideas
• Plants can _____ . That might be a good topic.	• I think/do not think that is a good topic because _____ .
• I know a lot about _____ , so I'll write about that.	• _____ sounds interesting. Tell me more.
• My favorite plant is _____ . I would like to say more about it.	• I like that plant, too. I would like to read about _____ .

2. **Gather Information** Find all the facts and details you'll need for your article. Do they all tell about the same topic?

3. **Get Organized** Use a main idea and details diagram to help you organize what you'll say.

Main Idea and Details Diagram

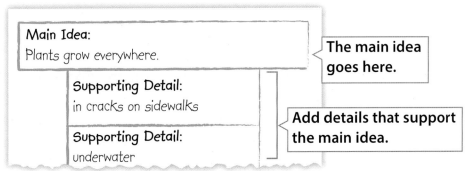

Main Idea:
Plants grow everywhere.

The main idea goes here.

Supporting Detail:
in cracks on sidewalks

Supporting Detail:
underwater

Add details that support the main idea.

Draft

Use your main idea and details diagram to write your draft.

• Turn your main idea into a topic sentence.

• Turn your details into sentences that tell more about the main idea.

Revise

1. **Read, Retell, Respond** Read your draft aloud to a partner. Your partner listens and retells what your article is about. Next, talk about ways to improve your writing.

Language Frames	
Retell • The topic is _____ . • Most of the facts and details tell about _____ .	**Make Suggestions** • The detail about _____ does not tell about _____ . Can you take out that detail? • I like the examples you used to tell about _____ .

2. **Make Changes** Think about your draft and your partner's suggestions. Then use revision marks to make your changes.

   • Delete details that don't tell about the topic or support the main idea.

   > Did you know that seeds can sprout in tiny cracks on sidewalks? ~~There are many plants near my house.~~

   • Add details or examples that support your main idea and keep your writing focused.

   > Some daisies, for example, grow big enough to break the pavement!
   > Did you know that seeds can sprout in tiny cracks on sidewalks?

Spelling Tip

To make most nouns plural, add **-s** or **-es**. For most nouns ending in **y**, change **y** to **i** and add **-es**.

Edit and Proofread

Work with a partner to edit and proofread your article. Check the spelling of plural nouns. Use revision marks to show your changes.

Present

1. **On Your Own** Make a final copy of your article. Then choose a way to share it with your classmates. You might want to read your article aloud, or you can just retell it from memory.

Presentation Tips	
If you are the speaker...	**If you are the listener...**
Speak slowly and clearly.	Take notes to help you understand and remember.
Provide more details if your listeners do not understand what you thought was amazing.	Make inferences based on what you know.

2. **With a Group** Work with your classmates to put all the articles into a science magazine. Make several copies to share with others in your school. You can post your magazine online, or turn it into a series of web pages.

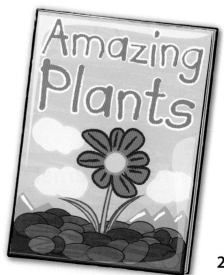

? BIG Question

What is so amazing about plants?

Talk Together

In this unit, you found lots of answers to the **Big Question**. Now, use your concept map to discuss the **Big Question** with the class.

Concept Map

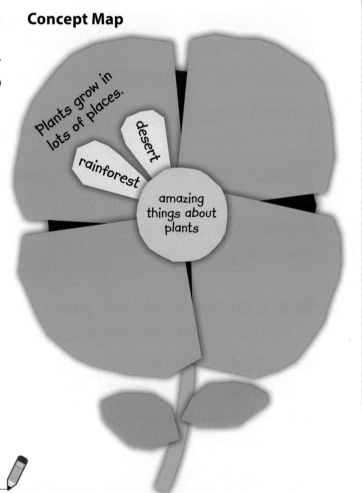

Plants grow in lots of places.

rainforest

desert

amazing things about plants

Write a Journal Entry 🖊

Choose one amazing thing about plants from your concept map. Write a journal entry about it.

Share Your Ideas

Choose one of these ways to share your ideas about the **Big Question**.

Write It!

Make a Cartoon

Draw a cartoon about an amazing plant. Write a caption to show what is so amazing about the plant. Explain your cartoon to the class.

This plant eats bugs!

Talk About It!

Talk Show

Choose classmates to talk about each selection in this unit. Each guest on the talk show gives amazing information they have learned about plants. Use formal language.

Do It!

Perform a Skit

Write a skit about people who work with plants. Show why the people think plants are amazing. Decide whether to use formal or informal language. Perform your skit for the class.

Write It!

Plant Poem

Think about your favorite plant. Write a haiku about it. Count the syllables in each line. Then read your poem aloud to a partner.

Let's Work Together

BIG Question

What's the best way to get things done?

CORBY, United Kingdom
A pit crew working on a race car during a pit stop

Unit at a Glance
▷ **Language Focus**: Express Needs, Wants, and Feelings; Persuade
▷ **Reading Strategy**: Determine Importance, Summarize
▷ **Phonics Focus**: Syllable Division, Vowel Sounds and Spellings: *al, aw, au*
▷ **Topic**: Working Together

Share What You Know

Do It!

❶ **Sketch** people doing a job. Put your pictures face down in a pile.

❷ **Take** turns drawing a picture. Begin to pantomime the job.

❸ **Have** classmates join in, one by one, to help pantomime the job. The rest of the class can try to guess the job at any time.

washing a car

Language Frames

- I need _____.
- I want _____.
- I feel _____.

Express Needs, Wants, and Feelings

Listen to Noah's song. Then use **Language Frames** to express needs, wants, and feelings of your own.

Song ♪

Everyone Helps

Oh, let's celebrate with a great big cake.
We'll play music on the trumpet and the drum.
But I need some help when I decorate
With flowers and balloons for everyone.

Everyone, everyone,
I want everyone to come.
If we work to help each other,
We can celebrate together.
I feel sure that our big party will be fun!

Tune: "Polly Wolly Doodle"

Congratulations, Team!

balloon

trumpet

drum

Balloons

Balloons

Congratulations Team!

Key Words

advertisement

buyer

market

money

pay

seller

🔊 Key Words

People go to a store or a **market** to buy food, party supplies, and other things they need. Use **Key Words** and other words to talk about the market in the picture.

How much does this cost?

You can **pay** me $3.50.

buyer

money

seller

advertisement

Buy fresh fruit at Joe's Market!

Talk Together

What's the best way to get things you need? Talk with a partner. Use **Key Words**. Then use Language Frames from page 222 to express your needs, wants, and feelings about the topic.

223

Thinking Map

Theme

A **theme** is the main message you get from a story or a situation. How do you figure out a theme? You use clues from the people, place, and events.

Look at these pictures of Noah's party. Read the text.

An Extra Guest

My sister Marty wants to join our party.

Let's make space for her.

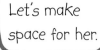

Welcome, Marty!

Thank you! This is fun.

Map and Talk

A theme chart can help you paraphrase a theme, or tell it in your own words. Here's how you make one.

Write details, or clues, in the squares. Use the clues to help you write a theme sentence.

Theme Chart

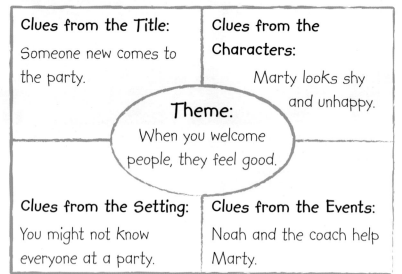

Clues from the Title:
Someone new comes to the party.

Clues from the Characters:
Marty looks shy and unhappy.

Theme:
When you welcome people, they feel good.

Clues from the Setting:
You might not know everyone at a party.

Clues from the Events:
Noah and the coach help Marty.

Tell your partner a story. Your partner makes a theme chart.

🔊 More Key Words

Use these words to talk about "I've Got This" and "Ba's Business."

accomplish
verb

To **accomplish** means to finish something that you want to do. What did she **accomplish**?

cooperation
noun

Cooperation is when people work together. It takes **cooperation** to row the boat quickly.

plenty
pronoun

When you have **plenty** of something, you have a lot of it. The picture shows **plenty** of fruit.

purpose
noun

A **purpose** is the reason for doing something. What is the **purpose** of writing a letter?

reward
noun

A **reward** is a gift or prize for doing something well. He gives the dog a **reward**.

Talk Together

Tell the meaning of a **Key Word** to a partner. Your partner uses the word in a sentence. Switch roles.

Plenty means a lot of something.

I have plenty of friends.

Learn to Determine Importance

Look at the picture. Which parts mean the most to you? When you figure out what is important to you, you **determine importance**.

When you read, you **determine what is important to you**, too.

How to Determine Importance

💭	**1.** Identify what the text is about.	This part is about _____.
💭	**2.** Decide on a **purpose** for reading.	I want to know more about _____.
👁	**3.** Focus on your purpose. Look for details that tell you what you want to know.	When I read _____, I learn _____.

Talk **Together**

Read the personal narrative. Read the sample determination. Then use **Language Frames** to determine what is important to you. Explain your thinking to a partner.

Personal Narrative

Balloons for Food

Our Little League team is planning a food drive. The **purpose** is to aid the homeless people in our city. We are working in **cooperation** with the **sellers** at the Farmer's **Market**. Many people have already bought food from the sellers to give to the drive. That will help us **accomplish** our goal of feeding the homeless.

"Will the donors get a **reward**?" asked Marty.

"What kind of reward?" asked Coach. "We can't **pay** a lot of **money** for rewards."

"Balloons!" said Marty. "You could order printed balloons that say 'Farmer's Market Food Drive' and give information about it."

Coach agreed. He paid 50 dollars for 200 printed balloons. "That should be **plenty**," he said.

On the day of the drive, he asked Marty to hand out the balloons. Marty untied the first balloon, and an entire bunch escaped! A dozen balloons sailed up into the air.

Coach just laughed. "Look at that!" he said, pointing to the bright spots in the sky. "Maybe we'll get more donors this way."

He was right. People found the balloons and brought more food to the drive.

> **Sample Determination**
>
> "This part is about a food drive.
>
> I want to know more about the food drive.
>
> When I read that the team is working with a farmer's market, I learn more about how the food drive will work."

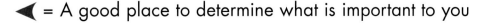
◄ = A good place to determine what is important to you

227

Phonics Focus

🔊 Syllable Division

dolphin = dol/phin = 2 syllables
VC/CCV

tiger = ti/ger = 2 syllables
VCV

Listen and Learn

🔊 Listen to each sentence. Choose the answer that shows the correct way to divide the bold word into syllables.

1. Write the **complete** address on the letter.

c/omplete
comp/lete
com/plete

2. We read a story about a silly **monster** that got into trouble.

mon/ster
monst/er
mons/ter

3. A **zebra** has stripes on its body.

zeb/ra
zebr/a
ze/bra

4. Write on the **paper**.

pap/er
pa/per
pape/r

🔊 Listen and read. Find the two-syllable words with vowel-consonant-vowel (VCV) and vowel-consonant-consonant-consonant-vowel (VCCCV) patterns.

Over to You

The Big Sale

"I need to earn some money. I love soccer and want to get a ticket to the soccer game," said Lucas.

"You have a lot of old things in your room. Why don't you sell some of them?" suggested Amy.

"Great idea!" said Lucas.

Amy helped Lucas make a flyer to attract buyers to his sale. On the day of the sale, Amy helped him drag a table into the yard and set it up. They put out the things Lucas planned to sell.

Amy held up a toy zebra with a missing leg. "Explain this to me," she said. "Who would pay for this broken toy?" She pointed to a basketball with no air in it. "Or this? It doesn't even bounce!"

"OK, maybe I should take some things out of the sale," said Lucas.

Amy helped Lucas sort out things that were broken or too old. That still left plenty of items he could sell.

Lucas sold almost everything he had put out. He accomplished his goal. There was more than enough money for his ticket.

"I feel I owe you a big thanks," said Lucas. As a reward for Amy's help, he got a ticket for her, too.

Work with a partner.

Write the words with VCV and VCCCV patterns. Work with a partner to divide the words into syllables.

◀ Practice reading words with vowel-consonant-vowel (VCV) syllables and vowel-consonant-consonant-consonant-vowel (VCCCV) syllables by reading "The Big Sale" with a partner.

Read a Realistic Story

Genre

This story tells about something that could really happen. It is **realistic fiction**.

Third-Person Narrator

The person who tells a story is the narrator. A third-person narrator uses the words *he*, *she*, and *they* to describe the action in the story.

Manuel

Rosie

I've Got This

by Susan Henderson

▶ **Set a Purpose**
Find out what happens when
Manuel tries to surprise his dad
by making a birthday cake.

It was Dad's birthday, but Manuel didn't have enough **money** to buy a present, so he decided to bake him a cake. *I'll make a chocolate cake*, he thought. *Chocolate is Dad's* **favorite**.

But Manuel had never baked a cake before. He found a cookbook with a **recipe** for chocolate cake and started **rounding up** the ingredients he would need.

favorite what he likes the most
recipe instructions for how to cook
    something
rounding up gathering

Manuel went to the **cupboard** where the flour was **stored**. He took out the bag, a box of sugar, and cocoa.

"What are you doing?" asked Manuel's sister, Maria. "Making a cake for Dad's birthday," he answered.

"Can I help?" she asked.

"No, **I've got this**," said Manuel as he turned back to the book. "Let's see . . . we need a **whisk**. Do we have a whisk?"

Maria got the whisk out from a drawer and handed it to her brother. "Yep, you've got this," she said as she left the kitchen.

cupboard cabinet
stored kept
I've got this I can do it
whisk utensil to beat or whip food like
    eggs or cream

Manuel's brother, Luis, came into the kitchen. He saw his brother bringing a carton of milk and **a dozen** eggs to the **counter**.

"Can I help?" asked Luis.

"No thanks, I've got this," said Manuel. Then he tried to crack one of the eggs into the bowl, but the egg cracked in his hand instead.

Luis handed him a towel. "Here you go, Manny." As he left the kitchen, he looked back and said to his brother, "Yeah, you've got this."

a dozen twelve
counter a flat surface
    to prepare food

Manuel cleaned himself up and went back to making the cake. Just then, a little voice from below said **meekly**, "I help?" He turned to see his little sister looking up at him with big, hopeful eyes.

"Thanks, Rosie, but you're too little to help," Manuel told her.

Rosie began to **wail**. It was hard to believe such a loud noise could come out of such a small person.

"OK, OK," said Manuel. "You can help, Rosie."

meekly timidly, quietly
wail cry loudly

Manuel lifted Rosie onto a high chair. She grabbed an egg, but he snatched it back before Rosie had a chance to crack it.

"Here, Rosie," he said, "you can have this spoon." He returned to work on the cake and didn't see Rosie grabbing a stick of butter.

Rosie took the wrapping off the butter. By the time Manuel **looked up**, it was too late. Rosie had spread the butter all over her face.

"Listen, Rosie," Manuel said as he cleaned her up, "if we're going to **accomplish** this before Dad gets home, I'm going to need some **cooperation** ."

looked up noticed

Manuel **set about** making the cake once more. He poured a cup of milk and then **sifted** the flour into a bowl. He didn't notice Rosie reaching for the milk. **The next thing he knew**, the milk was all over the counter and the floor.

"Rosie!" he said, "This is not the kind of **cooperation** I was hoping for!"

Manuel didn't see Maria and Luis watching from the doorway.

set about doing something in a determined way
sifted strained to remove lumps
The next thing he knew When he realized what was happening

▶ Before You Continue

1. **Make Inferences** How does Manuel feel about his brother and sister helping him make the cake? How can you tell?

2. **Point of View** Is the narrator a character in the story? How do you know?

▶ **Predict**
What do you think Manuel will
do to have his dad's cake ready
in time?

"**R**osie, please stop helping!" **exclaimed** Manuel.
"I have to hurry, or I'll never have Dad's cake ready **in time**!"

Manuel bent down to clean up the spilled milk. But while
he was doing that, Rosie reached for the bag of flour. Manuel
stood up just in time to see her turning the bag of flour upside
down over her head.

"I help!" she said as she giggled.

Manuel slumped. Just then, Maria and
Luis came into the kitchen.

exclaimed cried out
in time when he comes home

"Hey, big brother," said Maria smiling. "You still *got* this?"

"Looks like you could use some help," said Luis.

"Well, I'd be done by now if Rosie didn't keep . . . helping," said Manuel.

"Oh, so you don't need our help?" asked Maria. "OK, we'll go then."

As Luis and Maria turned to leave, Manuel said **sheepishly**, "Please don't go. Yes, I need your help."

sheepishly shyly, meekly

Maria **dusted off** Rosie and they all went to work.

Luis added cocoa to the flour. Manuel added eggs to the butter and sugar. Then he reached for the container of milk. It was empty.

"Oh no!" he cried. "We're **out of milk**—Rosie spilled the last cup."

"No problem," said Luis. "I'll run to the **market** and get some more."

"Please hurry," said Manuel. "We have to get this cake in the oven, or it won't be ready by the time Dad gets home from work."

dusted off cleaned up
out of milk no longer have any milk

Luis quickly returned from the **market** with the milk. Then the **siblings** got **back to the business** of making their dad's birthday cake.

Maria added the milk to the butter and sugar mixture. Luis slowly poured in the flour. Then Luis, Maria, and Manuel took turns mixing up the **batter**.

Rosie waved a mixing spoon in the air. And she didn't spill anything.

siblings brothers and sisters
back to the business to work again
batter mixture that will become cake

▶ **Before You Continue**

1. **Confirm Prediction** What does Manuel do? Was your prediction correct?

2. **Determine Importance** What important things do the characters say or do? Why are they important?

▶ **Predict**
What else will the kids do to make their dad's birthday special?

Finally, the batter was ready. Manuel put the pan in the oven and set the timer. Then Luis, Maria, and Manuel cleaned up.

Maria said, "I have an idea. I still have some balloons and streamers left over from a school party. Let's **put them up**."

The kids agreed that was a great idea. They got to work decorating the apartment.

Rosie traced pictures with her finger in the flour that was left on the floor.

put them up decorate

It seemed to take **forever** for the cake to be finished.
Finally, *Ding!* went the oven timer. The family crowded
around as Manuel pulled the cake from the oven.

"How did it come out?" asked Luis nervously.

"It looks perfect," said Maria.

"I think you're right, Maria," said Manuel. They all
leaned in and inhaled the smell of the cake. It smelled sweet
and sugary.

"*We've* got this," said Maria smiling.

forever a very long time

The kids were so excited when their dad finally walked through the door that afternoon.

"Happy Birthday, Dad!" exclaimed Maria and Luis **in unison**.

Dad loved his cake. "Wow!" he said. "What a nice surprise. How did you ever **accomplish** this?"

"It wasn't easy, but we all worked together," said Manuel.

"I help," said Rosie.

"Yes, Rosie," laughed Manuel. "You were the biggest help of all!" ❖

in unison together

▶ Before You Continue

1. **Confirm Prediction** Was your prediction correct? Explain.

2. **Theme** What is the theme of the story? Give details from the story to support your ideas.

Susan Henderson

Susan Henderson has three sisters. She is the oldest and remembers how her youngest sister, who is 12 years younger, always wanted to tag along and help. When Susan grew up, she went to live in Australia and learned how to make delicious Australian desserts. Her favorite was pavlova covered in mango and passion fruit.

Susan now lives in Seattle, but she still loves pavlova!

◀ **birthday cake**

◀ **pavlova**

Writing Tip

The author uses dialogue to help you understand the characters. Imagine that Manuel wants to cook something else. What would he say to his brother and sisters? What would they say to him? Write their dialogue. Use words that sound like something the characters would say.

Talk About It

Key Words

accomplish	pay
advertisement	plenty
buyer	purpose
cooperation	reward
market	seller
money	

1. Compare this story to another **realistic** story you know. How are they the same?

They are the same because _____.

2. Manuel wants to do everything on his own. Pretend you are Maria or Luis. **Express needs, wants, and feelings** about the situation.

I need _____. I want _____. I feel _____.

3. What does Manuel mean when he says, "I've got this"? In the end Maria says "We've got this!" Who was right? Why? What lesson does Manuel learn?

When Manuel says, "I've got this," he means _____. I think Manuel / Maria was right because _____. Manuel learns _____.

Write About It

Why do you think Manuel didn't want to have much **cooperation** with his siblings at first? How did this change as the story went on? Write two sentences to explain how Manuel felt at the beginning of the story and two sentences to explain how he felt at the end. Use **Key Words** to help explain your responses.

At the beginning of the story, Manuel didn't want to cooperate because _____.

At the end of the story, he _____.

Theme

Make a theme chart for "I've Got This." Locate details, or clues, in different parts of the story. Then use the clues to help you write, or paraphrase, a theme sentence.

Theme Chart

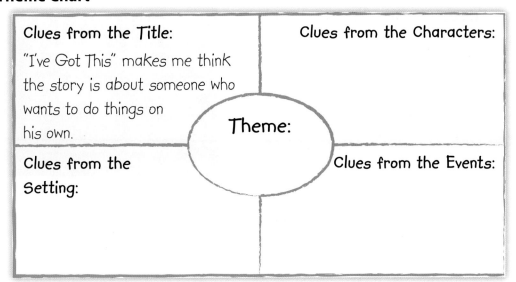

Clues from the Title:	Clues from the Characters:
"I've Got This" makes me think the story is about someone who wants to do things on his own.	
Clues from the Setting:	Clues from the Events:

Theme:

Work with a partner. Discuss your theme sentence and the details that support it. Use the sentence frames and **Key Words**. Record your discussion.

This clue _____ .
This clue _____ .
So the theme is: _____ .

Fluency

Practice reading with intonation. Rate your reading.

Talk Together

What's the best way to surprise someone on their birthday? Write what Manuel would say. Use at least one **Key Word**. Read Manuel's words to a partner.

Prefixes

A **prefix** is a word part that comes at the beginning of a word. A prefix changes the meaning of the word.

How does the word **market** change? Look at this example.

The prefix **super**- means "larger than" or "superior to."

super- + market = supermarket

A **supermarket** is a very large market.

Try It Together

Read the sentences. Then answer the questions.

We did not have to wait in line at the movie. We had <u>prepurchased</u> our tickets. When we got popcorn, my friend paid for me. "I'll <u>repay</u> you tomorrow," I said.

1. **The prefix pre- means "before" or "in front of." What does prepurchased mean?**

   A purchased a lot

   B purchased after

   C purchased before

   D purchased quickly

2. **The prefix re- means "back" or "again." What does repay mean?**

   A pay back

   B pay after

   C pay more

   D pay before

Making Connections Read to find out more about how working together can have good results.

Genre This story tells about events that could really happen. It is **realistic fiction**.

◀) Ba's Business

*written and illustrated by **Grace Lin***

Ba was selling *daan taht* at the **street fair**. Hannah and Rose knew that their father's sweet egg tarts were delicious, but no one stopped at the **booth**.

"Business is very bad today," Ba sighed and shook his head sadly.

Ba Dad (in Chinese)
street fair outdoor market
booth table where they sold food

▶ **Before You Continue**

1. **Point of View** What words tell you this story has a third-person narrator?
2. **Clarify** What does *daan taht* mean? What clues help you understand the meaning?

"Maybe we can make it better," Hannah whispered to Rose.

So Hannah made a large sign and Rose **offered free samples**.

People lined up to try the small pieces of *daan taht*.

"This is delicious!" everyone said. "I have to buy some for my family!"

offered free samples gave people free pieces of *daan taht* to try

By the end of the day, Ba had sold **every last** *daan taht*.

"Business was very good today!" Hannah and Rose said to Ba.

Ba nodded and **grinned** at his daughters.

"With your help," he said, as he put an arm around each girl, "our business will be good every day." ❖

every last all of the
grinned smiled

▶ **Before You Continue**

1. **Determine Importance** Look back at the text. What part of the story is most important to you? Why?
2. **Theme** What is the theme of the story? Use details from the text to support your ideas.

251

Key Words	
accomplish	pay
advertisement	plenty
buyer	purpose
cooperation	reward
market	seller
money	

Compare Characters

In the stories, both Manuel and Ba change how they act. What are the characters like when the stories begin? How do they act at the end? Make a comparison chart with a partner.

Comparison Chart

	Beginning of story	End of story	Why does the character change?
Manuel	He wants to do everything on his own.		
Ba			

Now use your chart to describe the interactions of the characters, or how they act with one another. What does Manuel learn from his brother and sisters? How do Ba and his daughters act? What is their relationship?

Talk Together

What is the best way to have a meal together or to sell food? Look back at the selections. Use **Key Words** to talk about your ideas.

Present-Tense Action Verbs

A **present-tense action verb** tells about an action that is happening now. The verb must agree with the subject.

Grammar Rules Present-Tense Action Verbs	
• Use **-s** at the end of an action verb if the subject is **he**, **she**, or **it**.	Manuel **works** with his siblings. He **works** with his siblings. Rosie **helps** Manuel. She **helps** Manuel. The cake **tastes** delicious. It **tastes** delicious.
• Do not use **-s** for **I**, **you**, **we**, or **they**.	I **cook** with my dad. We **wash** the dishes together.

Read Present-Tense Action Verbs

Read these sentences about Manuel and Rosie. Identify three action verbs. Spell the verbs. Name the subjects.

Rosie helps Manuel make the cake. She spills the milk. Manuel cleans it up.

Write Present-Tense Action Verbs

Write two sentences about the characters. Use present-tense action verbs. Make sure the verbs agree with the subjects. Read your sentences to a partner.

Language Frames

• You/we must _____ .
• You/we should
  _____ .
• You/we could _____ .

Persuade

Listen to Clara's chant. Then use **Language Frames** to persuade classmates about an idea you have.

Chant

A Healthy Idea

We must eat our vegetables—
Three vegetables a day.
So we should grow a garden here.
Let's do it right away!

We could plant this plot of dirt
With vegetables and herbs.
All those vitamins and minerals
Will make us feel superb!

You should plant a garden, too.
It's a healthy thing to do.

🔊 Key Words

Look at the pictures. Use **Key Words** and other words to talk about **agriculture**.

Key Words

agriculture

crop

farmer

field

harvest

plow

1.

Farmers plow the land.

2.

They plant seeds in their **fields**.

3.

They water the plants.

4.

They **harvest** their **crops**.

Talk Together

What's the best way to do the work on a farm? Use **Language Frames** from page 254 and **Key Words**. Try to persuade your partner to agree with you.

Opinion and Evidence

When you give an **opinion**, you tell what you believe about something. You might say:

- In my opinion, ____ .
- I think ____ .

Read Clara's opinion and supporting reasons, or **evidence**.

I think my neighbors and I should plant our own vegetables.

Celery $1.35

Our vegetables will be fresher. They'll cost less. Gardening is good exercise, too.

Map and Talk

You can use an opinion chart to record an opinion and the evidence that supports it. To make one, write the opinion in the top box. List each piece of evidence under the top box.

Opinion Chart

> **Opinion:**
> I think we should plant our own vegetables.

>> **Evidence:**
>> Our vegetables will taste fresher.
>>
>> **Evidence:**
>> They will cost less money.
>>
>> **Evidence:**
>> Gardening is good exercise.

Talk Together

Tell your partner an opinion that you have. Give supporting reasons. Your partner makes an opinion chart.

◀) More Key Words

Use these words to talk about "A Better Way" and "The Ant and the Grasshopper."

alternative
noun

An **alternative** is another choice. An apple is a healthy **alternative** to candy.

conservation
noun

Conservation means the opposite of waste. **Conservation** of water is important.

future
noun

The **future** is what will happen tomorrow or sometime after that. My birthday is in the **future**.

method
noun

A **method** is a way of doing something. Is using your fingers to count a good **method**?

sustain
verb

To **sustain** means to keep something or someone alive or in existence.

Talk Together

Write a sentence for each **Key Word**. Use context clues. Put a blank for the **Key Word**. A partner fills in the word.

> We give the plants food to _____ them.

257

Learn to Summarize

Look at the picture. What does it show? Determine which parts are important. Then think of a sentence or two to briefly tell, or **summarize**, what the picture shows.

Basil

Peppermint

When you read, you can **summarize**, too.

How to Summarize

1. Identify the topic.

2. Take notes as you read. Jot down important details.

3. Use your notes to retell the important ideas in your own words.

This part is about _____ .

I should remember _____ .

This part _____ .

Talk Together

Read the speech. Identify what Clara wants the reader to do. Then read the sample summary. Use **Language Frames** to summarize parts of the text.

Persuasive Speech

Window Dressing

This week, my mom and I planted two herb boxes outside our kitchen windows. I think everyone should have herb boxes. They have so many benefits. Today, I'm going to tell you what some of those benefits are.

First, herb boxes are tiny gardens. They are easy to plant and to **sustain**. All you need is a container full of planting soil, seedlings, sunlight, and water. You don't need much water either. These tiny gardens are great for water **conservation**.

Fresh herbs are also great for cooking. Mom's spaghetti topped with basil sauce is the best! Freshly grown herbs give cooks a wonderful **alternative**. They are always handy. Sure, you can buy herbs in a bottle. But these are never as fresh as the herbs you grow yourself. It's the best **method**. ◀

Finally, herb gardens smell wonderful! Sweet, sharp smells float on the air. Herb gardens look pretty, too. Imagine all those tiny green leaves outside your window. ◀

As I prepared this speech, I hoped that I could persuade you to plant herbs. I really hope that each of you has your own herb garden in the **future**.

Sample Summary

"This part is about planting an herb garden. I should remember the things you need.

This part says that you just need soil, seedlings, sunlight, and a little water for an herb garden."

◀ = A good place to summarize

Vowel Sounds and Spellings: al, aw, au

chalk

paw

launch

Listen and Learn

Listen to each sentence. Choose the word that best completes the sentence.

1. I need to add _____ to the stew.

sand   sight   salt

2. The bank keeps money in a _____.

vat   vault   vest

3. We watched a _____ fly high in the sky.

heart   hunk   hawk

4. We saw the rocket _____.

lunch   launch   latch

🔊 Listen and read. Find the words with the vowel sound you hear in the word *saw*.

An Island in Trouble

The small island of Kokota lies off the coast of East Africa. People on the island once made their living from cutting trees and selling lumber. They cut down almost all of the trees. Losing the trees caused big problems. Without tree roots, the soil couldn't hold water. It turned to dust.

A man on a nearby island thought he had the answer. "You must grow trees," he said. He launched a program to grow trees. He showed the people of Kokota how to build water tanks to catch rain water. Then they planted many trees.

Agriculture on the island has changed. People can now draw water from water tanks to grow nuts, fruit trees, and other crops. Thanks to its conservation methods, the island of Kokota has a good future.

Work with a partner.
Point to a word with the vowel sound you hear in the word *saw* and have your partner say it.

◀ Practice reading words with the vowel sound you hear in the word *saw* by reading "An Island in Trouble" with a partner.

Read a Persuasive Article

Genres

A **persuasive article** states an opinion about an issue and gives evidence to support it.

Text Features

Text is divided into parts called **sections**. A **section heading** tells what a section is about.

section heading

A New Solution

section

Paola Segura and Cid Simões, who live in Brazil, have a different solution. They agree that we need to help save trees. But they believe that we need to help people, too. They think that the way to help the Earth and the farmers is to use a way of farming. It is called "sustainable agriculture."

A Better Way

by Juan Quintana

NATIONAL
GEOGRAPHIC
EXCLUSIVE

263

▸ **Set a Purpose**
Learn about a **method** of farming
that helps both the land and
people.

Losing Trees

Every year, many **acres** of Earth's precious forests are cut down.
Sometimes people cut down the forest for wood. Other times,
they cut it down to make room for **cattle** or large farms. Often,
poor **farmers** burn a small area of forest to **clear it of** trees. In
the cleared area, they plant **crops** to feed their families. This is
called **slash**-and-burn **agriculture**.

Slash-and-Burn Agriculture

1. **Farmers** cut down trees.

2. **Farmers burn the dry
   trees to clear the land.**

3. **Farmers plant crops.
   When the land wears
   out, they clear new land.**

acres large areas
cattle cows
clear it of get rid of the
slash cut

For all of these reasons, forests have been disappearing. Some people blame humans. They think farming is the problem. To them, the solution is clear. People should stay out of the forest. **Farming must be limited!**

▼ **crops** planted in a forest

Farming must be limited!
People must not farm too much!

▶ **Before You Continue**

1. **Summarize** In your own words, retell the important ideas in this section.
2. **Steps in a Process** What is the second step in slash-and-burn **agriculture**? Point to where you found the information.

A New Solution

Paola Segura and Cid Simões, who live in Brazil, have a different solution. They agree that we need to help save trees. But they believe that we need to help people, too. They think that the way to help the Earth and the **farmers** is to use a way of farming. It is called "sustainable **agriculture** ."

BRAZIL
SOUTH AMERICA
NATIONAL GEOGRAPHIC

▲ Segura and Simões were named "Emerging Explorers" by the National Geographic Society. The Society wanted to thank them for their work.

Segura and Simões met in Costa Rica at Earth University. There they studied sustainable agriculture. They believe that farmers can earn money from a small piece of land. They can live there and **raise** their families. They can have healthy land and a community that **lasts**.

Using sustainable **agriculture**, **farmers** use the same small piece of land over and over again to grow **crops**. That way, they don't have to find new land and cut down more forests.

raise take care of
lasts stays together for a long time

▶ **Before You Continue**

1. **Use Text Features** Does the heading on page 266 give you a good idea of what this section is about? Explain.
2. **Summarize** Tell a partner the most important ideas on this page.

Helping Farmers

Today, Segura and Simões teach **farmers** about **crops** that grow well in the forest. Fruit trees and flowers can provide a good **income**. Fruit trees don't have to be replanted every year. Their deep roots help keep water and healthy nutrients in the soil. Some flowers, such as orchids, grow on less land than other crops. Farmers can sell their flowers to markets around the world.

People like to buy beautiful flowers. These are orchids. ▶

▲ Inside the fruit of a cocoa tree are seeds. The seeds can be sold to make chocolate.

income way to make money

Branching Out

To make a difference, many **farmers** need to grow **crops** this way. Segura and Simões use a special plan to teach more farmers. It is called the *5 × 5 System*. First, they teach one family how to grow crops that don't ruin the land. Then that family teaches five new families what they learned. Each new family teaches five more families. Think of all the land that could be saved in the **future**!

5 × 5 System

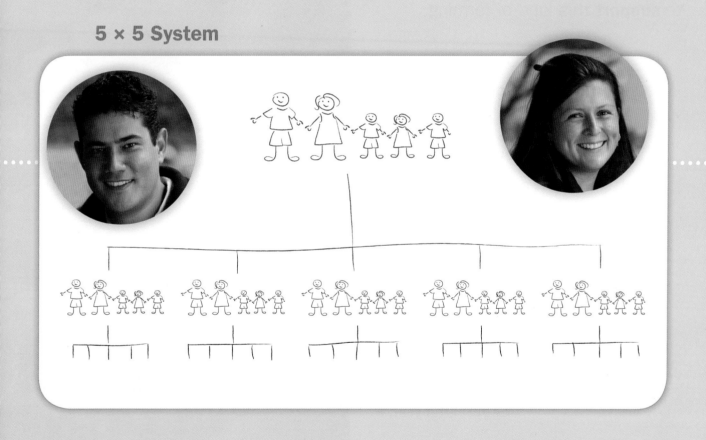

▶ **Before You Continue**
1. **Details** What are two types of sustainable **crops** for a forest?
2. **Summarize** Explain briefly in your own words how the 5 × 5 System works.

Let's Help Farmers Save Land!

Sustainable **agriculture** is good for the **farmer**. It is also good for the land. Here are three reasons why you should **support** this kind of farming.

First, sustainable agriculture lets farmers grow **crops** on the same land year after year. This is much better than slash-and-burn agriculture. When farmers stay on the same land, they build strong communities.

Palm hearts like these can grow on the same tree year after year. ▶

support help

Soybeans are a high-value **crop**. ▶

▲ Orchids grow naturally in the forest.

Secondly, sustainable **agriculture** is better for the forest. **Farmers** don't need to clear new land every year. Instead, they can grow **high-value crops**. That way, they can make money from a small amount of land. Some crops grow right in the forest. Farmers don't have to clear any land at all!

high-value crops crops that are grown easily that people will always buy

▶ **Before You Continue**

1. **Opinion/Evidence** What is the author's opinion about slash-and-burn **agriculture**? How do you know?

2. **Use Text Features** Look at the photos. Name two plants that help save land.

Finally, sustainable **agriculture keeps farmers farming**. Every year, many poor farmers leave the land. They move to the city. This causes problems, such as **unemployment**. It also leaves the land without people to care for it.

▲ **If they can't farm, some farmers have to move to the city to find work.**

keeps farmers farming lets farmers continue to farm

unemployment too few jobs for people in the city

To save forests and help **farmers**, we must support people like Paola Segura and Cid Simões. We must be part of the sustainable way of farming. What can you do to help? ❖

◀ **unshelled Brazil nuts**

▲ Brazil nuts can be a sustainable **crop**.

▶ **Before You Continue**

1. **Author's Purpose** What is the author's purpose for writing the article? How do you know?
2. **Cause and Effect** According to the text, what can happen when **farmers** are not able to keep farming?

Talk About It

1. Do you think this was a strong **persuasive article**? Give two reasons to support your opinion.

It was/was not strong because _____ .

2. Imagine you are a **farmer**. What is the best farming **method**? **Persuade** another farmer. Use evidence from the article.

The best method is _____ because _____ .

3. What kind of people are Paola Segura and Cid Simões? Tell about their personalities and ideas.

Segura and Simões are _____ . They _____ .

Write About It

Segura and Simões teach farmers about an **alternative** farming method. What are some benefits of this kind of farming to the whole community? Write two sentences. Use **Key Words** to explain your ideas.

One benefit is _____ .
Another benefit is _____ .

Opinion and Evidence

Make an opinion chart for pages 270–273 in "A Better Way."
Identify what the author is trying to persuade people to think
or do. List the supporting reasons, or evidence.

Opinion Chart

Opinion: **Sustainable agriculture** is good for the
farmer and good for the land.

Evidence: It lets farmers grow **crops**
on the same land year after year.

Now use your opinion chart to
explain the author's opinion and
evidence to a partner. Use the
sentence frames and **Key Words**.
Record your explanation.

The author thinks _____ .
One piece of evidence is _____ .
Another reason is _____ .

Fluency

Practice phrasing as you read. Rate your reading.

Talk Together

What's the best way to grow **crops**? Give a persuasive talk to
a group of classmates. State your opinion and give at least two
reasons to support it. Use **Key Words**.

Classify Words

You can group, or **classify**, words that tell about the same topic. This gives you a deeper understanding of the topic.

Look at this example. How does classifying help you understand the topic better?

Word Web

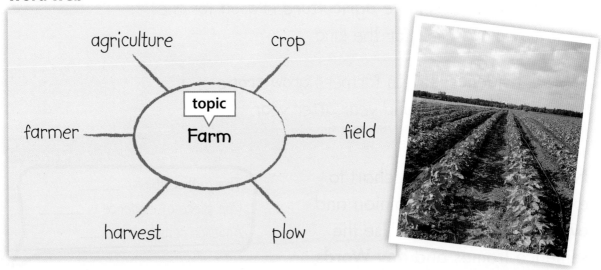

Try It Together

Read each item. Choose the correct answer.

1. **Which word does NOT belong in a group of words for the topic agriculture?**

   A land

   B seed

   C plant

   D ocean

2. **For the topic crop, add a word to this group of words: beans, nuts, _____ .**

   A fire

   B markets

   C potatoes

   D community

Making Connections Read more about how our actions today can affect the **future**.

Genre A **fable** is a story that teaches a lesson, or moral, about life. Many fables have animals as characters.

The Ant and the Grasshopper

an Aesop fable

retold by **Shirleyann Costigan**
illustrated by **Pablo Bernasconi**

One sunny day, a **merry** grasshopper was dancing to his fiddle. "**Watch your step!**" came a voice at his feet. It was an ant carrying **an enormous kernel** of corn.

fiddle

---

merry happy
"Watch your step!" "Be careful where you walk!"
an enormous kernel a big piece

▶ **Before You Continue**

1. **Ask Questions** What do you want to find out as you read? If you don't understand something, what will you do?
2. **Character** What is the grasshopper like? How do you know?

277

"Come dance with me!" **urged** the grasshopper.

"No time, no time," the ant answered without stopping.
"I must gather food for winter. Why aren't you gathering food?
It's a bad idea to wait until it snows."

"**Nonsense**," said the grasshopper. "Winter is a long time
away."

"**Suit yourself**," said the ant, and she **staggered forward**
under her heavy load.

---

urged said
Nonsense That's silly
Suit yourself Do what you want
staggered forward walked with difficulty

▶ **Before You Continue**

1. **Summarize** Reread this page. Say the
   ideas in your own words.
2. **Character** How do you think the ant and
   the grasshopper would describe each
   other? Explain.

Soon winter came, and snow covered the land. Not a kernel of food could be found. "Oh!" **lamented** the grasshopper. "I'm so hungry I **must surely** die!"

"Hey, Grasshopper!" cried a voice at his feet. It was the same ant. She was carrying another kernel of corn.

"I warned you this day would come," said the ant.

lamented cried
must surely am sure I will

"Yes, you did," **admitted** the grasshopper sadly. "And if I live to see another year, I will **heed your warning**."

"You'll live," said the ant, and she dropped the kernel in the snow. The grasshopper gratefully picked it up and began to eat.

And ever after, Grasshopper remembered the tiny ant's lesson and was never hungry again. ❖

Moral: *When someone tells you to save for the **future**, listen.*

admitted said
heed your warning listen to you
And ever after From then on

▶ **Before You Continue**

1. **Character** How does the ant help the grasshopper? How does Grasshopper change?

2. **Theme** Use your own words to tell the fable's moral, or lesson. Is the story a good example of the lesson? How?

Key Words

agriculture	future
alternative	harvest
conservation	method
crop	plow
farmer	sustain
field	

Compare Purposes

An author has a reason, or purpose, for writing. An author might write to:

- inform
- express feelings
- entertain
- persuade

What is the author's purpose in each selection? Make a comparison chart with a partner. Write the topic of each selection. Then locate the text in each selection that helps you understand the author's purpose. List the purpose. Can you write more than one purpose for each author?

Comparison Chart

Title: "A Better Way" by Juan Quintana	Topic: sustainable agriculture	Author's Purpose:
Title: "The Ant and the Grasshopper" by Shirleyann Costigan	Topic:	Author's Purpose:

Discuss the chart together. Do the authors share any purposes? Which purposes are different?

Talk Together

What's the best way to have enough land or food in the **future**? Think about the article and the fable. Use **Key Words** to talk about your opinions.

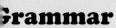

Forms of *be, have*

The verbs *be* and *have* have irregular forms. The subject and verb must agree. Look at the present-tense forms.

Grammar Rules Forms of *be/have*	be	have
• Use for **I**	am	have
• Use for **you**	are	have
• Use for **he**, **she**, and **it**	is	has
• Use for **we**	are	have
• Use for **they**	are	have

Read Forms of *be/have*

Read this passage based on "A Better Way." Find present-tense forms of *be* and *have*. Identify the subjects.

> A farmer has a small piece of land. He practices sustainable agriculture. It is a good farming method.

Write Forms of *be/have*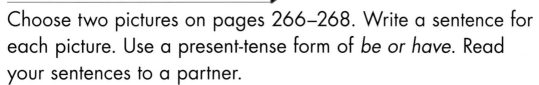

Choose two pictures on pages 266–268. Write a sentence for each picture. Use a present-tense form of *be or have*. Read your sentences to a partner.

Write as a Citizen

Write a Persuasive Essay

Write an essay about the best way to do something at school or in your neighborhood. You can present your opinion as a speech, then share it in a book or blog.

Study a Model

In a persuasive essay, you state your opinion and then give evidence to support it.

The first paragraph includes the writer's **opinion**.

Plant a Garden!

by Nick Wojtek

What's the best thing to do with an empty lot? In my opinion, you should make a neighborhood garden!

A neighborhood garden is a great idea for many reasons. First, it's a chance for neighbors to get to know each other.

Second, the garden gives people of all ages something to do. A garden always needs watering and weeding. Even little kids can help with that!

Finally, the garden is something everyone can enjoy. Flowers bloom all summer long. If you plant vegetables, you can eat them as they ripen.

So, if there's an empty lot in your neighborhood, plant a garden! You'll be happy that you did.

Evidence supports the opinion and develops the writer's ideas. The ideas are worthwhile and interesting.

The **end** restates the opinion. The writing feels complete.

Prewrite

1. **Choose a Topic** What do you want to persuade people to do? Talk with a partner to choose the best topic.

Language Frames	
Tell Your Ideas • I think the *best* way to _____ . • I think people should _____ . • I really believe _____ .	**Respond to Ideas** • Why do you think _____ is the best way? • I agree/disagree because _____ . • Let me see. You're saying _____ .

2. **Gather Information** What evidence, or reasons, can you give to support your opinion? What details or examples might help?

3. **Get Organized** Use an opinion chart to organize your ideas.

Opinion Chart

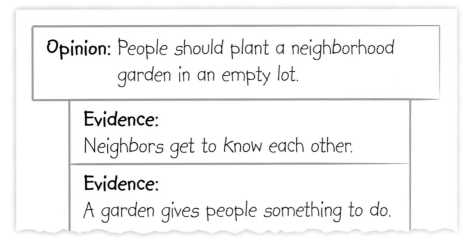

Opinion: People should plant a neighborhood garden in an empty lot.

Evidence:
Neighbors get to know each other.

Evidence:
A garden gives people something to do.

Draft

Use your opinion chart to help you write your draft.

• State your opinion in the first paragraph.

• Put each piece of evidence in a new paragraph.

• Explain your reasons with details and examples.

Revise

1. **Read, Retell, Respond** Read your draft aloud to a partner. Your partner listens and retells your opinion and evidence. Next, talk about ways to improve your writing.

Language Frames	
Retell	**Make Suggestions**
• Your opinion is _____ . • The reasons you give are _____ .	• I think you should state your opinion _____ . • Can you give a detail or example to help support _____ ?

2. **Make Changes** Think about your draft and your partner's suggestions. Then use revision marks to make your changes.

   • Make sure you include your opinion in the first paragraph.

   > What's the best thing to do with an empty lot?
   > ~~Neighborhood gardens are nice.~~ ∧In my opinion, you should make a neighborhood garden!

   • Do you develop your ideas with important details and examples? If not, add text.

   > Second, the garden gives people of all ages something to do. ~~Gardens take a lot of work.~~ ∧A garden always needs watering and weeding.

Edit and Proofread

Work with a partner to edit and proofread your persuasive essay. Pay special attention to subject-verb agreement. Use revision marks to show your changes.

Grammar Tip

✔ If the subject is **he**, **she**, or **it**, use **-s** at the end of an action verb in the present tense:
- The market open**s**.
- He buy**s** fruit.

Present

1. **On Your Own** Make a final copy of your persuasive essay. Present it as a speech to your classmates or to younger students. Ask them to share their responses when you are done.

Presentation Tips	
If you are the speaker...	**If you are the listener...**
Remember, you are persuading others. Keep your tone firm and confident.	Listen attentively for the speaker's opinion. Make sure you understand what it is.
Make eye contact to make sure your audience is listening.	Listen for the reasons and details the speaker uses to support his or her opinion.

2. **With a Group** Share your advice with others. Collect all the essays. Bind them into a book, and think of a good title for it. You could also start a weekly advice blog.

Talk Together

In this unit, you found lots of answers to the **Big Question**. Now, use your concept map to discuss the **Big Question** with the class.

Concept Map

work together

What's the best way to get things done?

Write a Description ✏️

Choose one of the ways on your concept map. Write a description of people using that method to get something done.

Share Your Ideas

Choose one of these ways to share your ideas about the **Big Question**.

Write It!

Write a Skit

Write a skit with a partner. Tell about a great way to protect trees or another part of nature. Decide whether to use formal or informal language. Perform your skit for the class.

Talk About It!

Be a Reporter

Have a partner pretend to be a character or person from the unit. Think of something you want to do, such as plant a vegetable garden. Use formal language to interview your partner about the best way to do this. Switch roles.

Do It!

Do a Chore Together

Think of a classroom chore, such as washing desktops. Have a group discussion to figure out the best way to do the chore. Ask questions and make comments. Then do the job!

Write It!

Write a Letter

Pretend that you have visited a city that recycles. Write a letter to a leader in your city. Tell how you think your community should recycle.

> April 5, 20_____
>
> Dear Mr. Reyes,
>
> I have just visited a city that recycles everything! I think our city should do that, too.

Picture Dictionary

The definitions are for the words as they are introduced in the selections of this book.

Parts of an Entry

The **entry** shows how the word is spelled.

The **picture** helps you understand more about the meaning of the word.

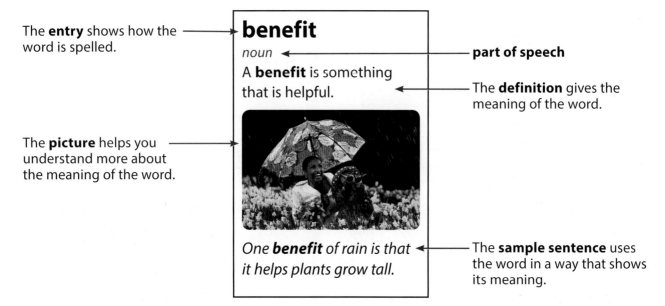

benefit

noun

A **benefit** is something that is helpful.

*One **benefit** of rain is that it helps plants grow tall.*

part of speech

The **definition** gives the meaning of the word.

The **sample sentence** uses the word in a way that shows its meaning.

A

accomplish
verb

To **accomplish** means to finish something that you want to do.

What did she accomplish?

action
noun

An **action** is something that you do.

Their actions made the park a clean place to play.

advertisement
noun

Advertisements can be photos, pictures, or even short movies that give information and try to make people buy things.

The advertisement made my dad want to buy that new car.

agriculture
noun

The work of growing crops and raising animals for people to eat is called **agriculture**.

Many people who live outside of cities and towns work in agriculture.

alternative
noun

An **alternative** is another choice.

An apple is a healthy alternative to candy.

amount
noun

The **amount** of something is how much of it there is.

Three hundred jelly beans is a large amount of candy.

B

balance
noun

When things are in **balance**, they are even.

The two sides of the scale are in balance.

a
b
c
d
e
f
g
h
i
j
k
l
m
n
o
p
q
r
s
t
u
v
w
x
y
z

behavior

noun

Behavior is what a person or animal does.

*Squirrels store nuts for the winter. It's part of their **behavior**.*

benefit

noun

A **benefit** is something that is helpful.

*One **benefit** of rain is that it helps plants grow tall.*

blossom

noun

A **blossom** is the flower of a seed plant.

*This **blossom** comes from an apple tree.*

buyer

noun

A **buyer** is someone who gets something by paying money for it.

*He wants a **buyer** for his flowers.*

characteristic

noun

A **characteristic** is how something looks or what something does.

*A **characteristic** of this plant is white flowers.*

city

noun

A **city** is a very large town.

*San Francisco is a large **city** in California.*

competition

noun

A **competition** is a contest or struggle between two or more people or animals.

*These pelicans are in **competition** for food.*

conditions

noun

When **conditions** are right, good things happen.

*Clear skies and wind are good **conditions** for sailing.*

conservation

noun

Conservation means the opposite of waste.

***Conservation** of water is important.*

control

verb

To **control** means to make a person or thing do what you want.

*The boys **control** where the car goes.*

cooperation

noun

Cooperation is when people work together.

*It takes **cooperation** to row the boat quickly.*

crop

noun

A **crop** is a large amount of plants a farmer grows, usually for food.

*This farm had a very large orange **crop** this year.*

cycle

noun

A **cycle** is a set of events that happen over and over again in a pattern.

*This diagram shows the life **cycle** of a frog.*

*This picture shows the life **cycle** of a butterfly.*

decrease

verb

When something **decreases** it becomes smaller in number, amount or in size.

*The amount **decreases** after each slice is taken away.*

a
b
c
d
e
f
g
h
i
j
k
l
m
n
o
p
q
r
s
t
u
v
w
x
y
z

depend
verb

To **depend** means to need something or someone for support.

*A baby **depends** on its mother.*

desert
noun

A **desert** is a hot, dry area where few plants grow.

*The **desert** gets very little rain.*

difference
noun

To make a **difference** is to make something better.

*They are making a **difference**. They are cleaning oil off the bird's body.*

diversity
noun

Diversity means a lot of different people or things.

*Our school has a great **diversity** of people.*

drought
noun

A **drought** is a long time of very dry weather.

*The river is dry because of a **drought**.*

duty
noun

When you do your **duty**, you do what you are supposed to do.

*The boy is doing his **duty** by throwing away his trash.*

ecosystem
noun

An **ecosystem** is a group of animals and plants, the place they live in, and how they act together.

*This alligator is part of this wetland's **ecosystem**.*

*This gila monster is part of this desert's **ecosystem**.*

environment
noun

Your **environment** is the kind of place where you live.

*This is a hot, dry **environment**.*

---

farmer
noun

A **farmer** is someone who grows crops or raises animals.

*The **farmer** picks carrots from the field.*

field
noun

A **field** is an open space of land, which is sometimes used to plant crops.

*This is a **field** of lettuce.*

*In some **fields**, farm animals eat grass.*

---

food chain
noun

A **food chain** is a series of animals and plants in which each one feeds on the one below it.

*Which fish in the cartoon stands for the "shark" in an ocean **food chain**?*

future
noun

The **future** is what will happen tomorrow or sometime after that.

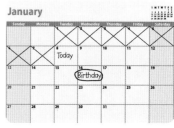

*My birthday is in the **future**.*

G

gift
noun

A **gift** is something you give to someone.

*An act of kindness can be a **gift**.*

growth
noun

The **growth** of something is how much bigger it gets.

*The ruler shows the **growth** of the plant.*

H

harvest
verb

When you **harvest**, you are gathering the crops that are ripe or ready to be picked.

*She **harvests** the ripe strawberries.*

I

identify
verb

When you **identify** something, you tell what it is.

*She wants to **identify** a type of bird.*

impact
noun

What you do has an **impact** on things.

*The children have a positive **impact** on the park.*

improve
verb

To **improve** something means to make it better.

*They **improve** the beach when they clean it.*

increase
verb

To **increase** means to grow in size or in number.

*When our dog eats too much food, its weight **increases**.*

individual
noun

An **individual** is one person.

*This **individual** is reading on her own.*

interact
verb

To **interact** means to act together.

*The students **interact** with each other to do a science project.*

kindness

noun

You show **kindness** when you are nice to someone.

*Teddy shows **kindness** to his mom.*

learn

verb

To **learn** means to find out how to do something.

*You can **learn** to play music.*

level

noun

The **level** of something is how high or low it is.

1/2 cup level

*The **level** of milk is one half cup .*

market

noun

A **market** is a place where people go to buy and sell food and other things.

*You can buy fruits and vegetables at this **market**.*

method

noun

A **method** is a way of doing something.

*Is using your fingers to count a good **method**?*

money

noun

Money is the coins and paper bills people use to buy things.

*This is enough **money** to buy a t-shirt.*

nature

noun

Nature means things like rivers, trees, and animals.

*She likes to study **nature**.*

need

verb

When you **need** something, you cannot live without it.

*People **need** to drink water.*

negative

adjective

Something that is **negative** is bad.

*Screaming at someone is a **negative** action.*

a
b
c
d
e
f
g
h
i
j
k
l
m
n
o
p
q
r
s
t
u
v
w
x
y
z

a b c d e f g h i j k l m **n** **o** **p** q r s t u v w x y z

neighborhood
noun

A neighborhood is the small area in a town around where a person lives.

*Children like to play in the **neighborhood**.*

O

offer
verb

An **offer** is saying you would like to help someone or give someone something.

*She **offers** food to her friend.*

organism
noun

An **organism** is a living thing.

insect

leaf

*This leaf and insect are both **organisms**.*

P

pay
verb

To **pay** is to give money for something.

*He will **pay** her for the sandwich.*

plenty
noun

When you have **plenty** of something, you have a lot of it.

*The picture shows **plenty** of fruit.*

plow
verb

To **plow** is to break up and turn over the soil in a field.

*Mules help farmers **plow** the fields.*

positive
adjective

Something that is **positive** is good for you.

*Exercise is a **positive** activity.*

problem
noun

A **problem** is a difficult situation that needs to be figured out.

*A broken toy is a **problem**.*

produce
verb

To **produce** means to make something.

*This factory **produces** cars.*

protect
verb
You **protect** something when you keep it safe.

spine

*Sharp spines **protect** the plant from animals.*

purpose
noun
A **purpose** is the reason for doing something.

*What is the **purpose** of writing a letter?*

rainforest
noun
A **rainforest** is a thick, tropical forest where a lot of rain falls.

***Rainforests** are home to lots of interesting wildlife.*

react
verb
When things happen, you usually **react** to them.

*The child **reacts** to the snowball.*

receive
verb
To **receive** is to get something from someone.

*She **received** my package in the mail today.*

resources
noun
Resources are things that you can use.

*A library has many **resources**.*

reward
noun
A **reward** is a gift or prize for doing something well.

*He gives the dog a **reward**.*

a b c d e f g h i j k l m n o **p** q **r** s t u v w x y z

299

river

noun

A **river** is a large, natural stream of water.

*This **river** runs through the land.*

root

noun

A **root** is the part of a plant that grows under the soil.

*People eat the **root** of the carrot plant.*

S

scarce

adjective

When something is **scarce**, it is hard to find or get.

*Food is **scarce** in this store.*

seed

noun

A **seed** is the small part of a plant from which a new plant can grow.

*This **seed** is beginning to grow.*

seller

noun

A **seller** is someone who has things people can buy.

*This **seller** has many carpets that you can buy.*

soil

noun

Soil is the dirt in which plants grow.

*The roots will grow in **soil**.*

solution

noun

A **solution** is the answer to a problem.

*His **solution** is to change the tire.*

sprout
noun

A **sprout** is a young plant or the new growth on a plant.

*These **sprouts** are growing out of the soil.*

supply
noun

A **supply** is the amount you have of something.

*They have a large **supply** of peaches.*

sustain
verb

To **sustain** means to keep something or someone alive or in existence.

*A mother bird brings food to **sustain** her chicks.*

understand
verb

When you **understand** something, you know what it means.

*Now he **understands** his homework.*

unique
adjective

Unique things are different from other things.

*The yellow flower is **unique**.*

*What is **unique** in this picture?*

value
verb

When you **value** something, you care about it.

*The girl loves and **values** her dog.*

vine
noun

A **vine** is a plant with a long stem that winds its way up trees or fences or runs along the ground.

vine

*The **vine** grows up the tree.*

volunteer
noun

A **volunteer** is someone who wants to help or do a job without being paid for it.

*This **volunteer** is helping to put away books.*

a b c d e f g h i j k l m n o p q r **s** t **u** **v** w x y z

want

verb

To **want** something is to hope or wish for it.

*He **wants** to get a guitar like this one.*

weed

noun

A **weed** is a wild plant that grows where it is not wanted.

dandelion

*These dandelions are **weeds**.*

Index

H

I

Index of Authors

Index of Illustrators

Text and Illustrator Credits

Unit One

Candlewick Press: Excerpt from *Those Shoes* by Maribeth Boelts, illustrated by Noah Z. Jones. Text copyright © 2007 by Maribeth Boelts. Illustrations © 2007 by Noah Z. Jones. Reproduced by permission of the publisher, Candlewick Press, Sommerville, Mass.

LEE & LOW BOOKS: From "Guardian Angel" by Francisco X. Alarcón from *Angels Ride Bikes*. Text Copyright © 2005 by Francisco X. Alarcón. Permission arranged with LEE & LOW BOOKS, Inc., New York, NY 10016. All rights not specifically granted herein are reserved.

Highlights for Children: Excerpt from "The World's Greatest Underachiever" by Henry Winkler from *Highlights for Children*, March 2005. Copyright © 2005 by Highlights for Children. Reprinted by permission of Highlights for Children, Inc.

Unit Two

Bloomsbury Publishing: Excerpt from *When the Wolves Returned* by Dorothy Hinshaw Patent. Text copyright © 2008 by Dorothy Hinshaw Patent. Photographs © 2008 by Dan Hartman and Cassie Hartman. Reprinted by permission of Bloomsbury Publishing. All rights reserved.

Photographic Credits

Cover C. Haessler/Shutterstock.com. iii (tl) Annie Griffiths (tr) zanskar/Getty Images (bl) Ami Vitale (br) David Madison/Getty Images. v Curt Wiler/Alamy Stock Photo. vii Don Johnston/Getty Images. ix Jabruson/Nature Picture Library. xi Carlos Alkmin/Getty Images. 2–3 Annie Griffiths. 4 anetapics/Shutterstock.com. 7 (tl) Ariel Skelley/Blend Images/Getty Images, (tc) Phovoir/Shutterstock, (tr) Hola Images/Getty Images, (bl) Don Mason/Blend Images/Getty Images, (bc) James Woodson/Photodisc/Getty Images. 10 (tl) Lana Langlois/Shutterstock.com, (tr) Tono Balaguer/Shutterstock.com, (cl) A3pfamily/Shutterstock, (cr) Kateryna Biatova/Shutterstock, (bl) Jordan Scanlan/Shutterstock, (br) donatas1205/Shutterstock. 11 Eva-Katalin/Getty Images. 30 (tl) RonTech2000/iStock/Getty Images, (tr) RonTech2000/iStock/Getty Images, (cr) DeeMPhotography/Shutterstock.com, (br) Print Collector/Getty Images. 36 Alfa Photostudio/Shutterstock. 37 Tim Pannell/Corbis/VCG/Getty Images, (tr) Alfa Photostudio/Shutterstock.com, (b) KidStock/Brand X Pictures/Getty Images. 39 (tl) Ariel Skelley/DigitalVision/Getty Images, (tc) charlybutcher/iStock/Getty Images, (tr) Shaun Egan/Photodisc/Getty Images, (bl) Fuse/Corbis/Getty Images (br) Stephen Simpson/The Image Bank/Getty Images. 42 (tl) gillmar/Shutterstock.com, (tc) Rick Wylie/Shutterstock.com, (tr) Napat/Shutterstock.com (cl) GreatStock/Masterfile, (cr) Pat_Hastings/Shutterstock.com, (br) oticki/Shutterstock. 43 Dragon Images/Shutterstock. 44–45 H. Armstrong Roberts/Retrofile/Getty Images. 46 (l) Jeff Morgan 07/Alamy Stock Photo (r) ZUMA Press, Inc./Alamy Stock Photo. 47 Harold M. Lambert/Getty Images. 50 Oleg Bonkovskyi/Shutterstock.com. 55 ABC Photo Archives/ABC via Getty Images. 56 AP Images/ROBERT BECKER (r) AP Images/Stefan Rousseau. 57 Fred Duval/FilmMagic/Getty Images. 61 (bkgnd) Curt Wiler/Alamy Stock Photo, (r) Suzannah Weiss. 62 (t) SV Photography /Alamy Stock Photo, (b) Carl & Ann Purcell/Corbis NX/Getty Images. 63 TT/Getty Images. 64 ton koene/Alamy Stock Photo. 65 Gideon Mendel/Corbis/Getty Images. 66 (l) H. Armstrong Roberts/Retrofile/Getty Images (r) Suzannah Weiss. 72 Annie Griffiths. 73 LightField Studios/Shutterstock.com. 74–75 zanskar/Getty Images. 79. (tl) icefront/iStock/Getty Images (tc)

Blend Images - Andersen Ross/Getty Images (tr) Yuriy Golub/Shutterstock.com (bl) quavondo/E+/Getty Images (bc) Samuel Aranda/Getty Images News/Getty Images. 82 (tl) wavebreakmedia/Shutterstock.com (tr) anaken2012/Shutterstock.com (cl) Eag1eEyes/Shutterstock.com (cr) wavebreakmedia/Shutterstock.com (bl) anaken2012/Shutterstock.com (br) photo one/Shutterstock.com. 83 Heiko Kiera/Shutterstock.com. 103 kridipol poolket/Shutterstock.com. 104 Red Squirrel/Shutterstock.com. 105 Jim Brandenburg/Minden Pictures/Superstock. 106 TessarTheTegu/Shutterstock.com. 107 Jeff Schultes/Shutterstock.com. 111 (t) by Mike Lyvers/Moment Open/Getty Images (b) Tim Graham/The Image Bank/Getty Images. 112 (l) davelogan/iStock/Getty Images (r) bierchen/Shutterstock.com. 113 (tl) ampower/Shutterstock.com (tc) JLBarranco/E+/Getty Images (tr) Zdravinjo/Shutterstock (bl) PhotoAlto/James Hardy/Getty Images/Houghton Mifflin Harcourt. (bc) Rob Marmion/Shutterstock.com. 114 ekawatchaow/Shutterstock.com. 115 Tashka/iStock/Getty Images. 116. (tl) MoreGallery/Shutterstock.com (tr) valzan/Shutterstock.com (cl) JIANG HONGYAN/Shutterstock.com (cr) Philographer/Shutterstock.com (bl) valzan/Shutterstock.com (br) Tong_stocker/Shutterstock.com. 117 Marc Schlossman/Getty Images. 118–119 imageBROKER/Alamy Stock Photo. 120 (l) Science History Images/Alamy Stock Photo (r) Max Studio/Shutterstock.com. 121 Don Johnston/Getty Images. 122 (tl) Bruce Raynor/Shutterstock.com (bl) mlorenzphotography/Getty Images. 122–123 Brian A Smith/Shutterstock.com. 124 ALAN CAREY/Science Source. 125 Stockox/Dreamstime.com. 126 Robert McGouey/Getty Images. 127 Peter Moulton/Shutterstock.com. 128–129 Barrett Hedges/Getty Images. 128 Nick Kuchera/Shutterstock.com. 130 (bl) Reimar Gaertner/UIG/Getty Images. 130–131 Sumio Harada/Minden Pictures. 132 (l) SERGEI BRIK/Shutterstock.com (r) Rostislav Stach/Shutterstock.com. 133 Christina Krutz/Getty Images. 134 miroslav chytil/Shutterstock.com 137 (inset) AP Images/Apichart Weerawong (bkgd) Asia Images Group Pte Ltd/Alamy Stock Photo 138 (bl) AP Images/Richard Vogel (br) AP Images/ZEB HOGAN (br) AP Images/ANDY EAMES. 139 Brian Atkinson/Alamy Stock Photo. 140 (t) Philippe Michel/AGE Fotostock (bl) Robert Nickelsberg/Time Life Pictures/Getty Images. 141 AP Images/Apichart Weerawong. 148 zanskar/Getty Images. 149 Khine/iStock/Getty Images. 150–151 Ami Vitale. 153 (t) Janis Smits/Shutterstock.com (tl) Brand X Pictures/Stockbyte/Getty Images (tr) Hayati Kayhan/Shutterstock.com (b) Johner Images/Alamy Stock Photo (br) VikaValter/iStock/Getty Images. 155 (tl) GFK-Flora/Alamy Stock Photo (tc) Teodor Ostojic/Shutterstock.com (tr) Kjuuurs/Shutterstock.com (bl) Walter B. McKenzie/The Image Bank/Getty Images (bc) Sandro Tucci/The LIFE Images Collection/Getty Images. 158 (tl) Kevin Oke/Getty Images (tr) Ingram Publishing/Alamy Stock Photo (tcl) aleksander hunta/Shutterstock.com (tcr) Image Republic/Shutterstock.com (bcl) Malochka Mikalai/Shutterstock.com (bcr) Ansis Klucis/Shutterstock.com (bl) real444/Getty Images (br) HelloRF Zcool/Shutterstock.com. 159 amenic181/Shutterstock.com. 176 (l) Brandon Blinkenberg/Shutterstock.com (r) Jiang Dao Hua/Shutterstock.com. 183 (t) Turnervisual/iStock/Getty Images (b) ranplett/iStock/Getty Images. 184 (tr) Michael & Patricia Fogden/Minden Pictures/Getty Images (bl) Siede Preis/Photodisc/Getty Images (br) Tim Fitzharris/Minden Pictures (tl) Hampton-Brown/National Geographic Image Collection (tr) Hampton-Brown/National Geographic Image Collection (bl) Hampton-Brown/National Geographic Image Collection (br) Hampton-Brown/National Geographic School Publishing. 185 (tl) HDesert/Shutterstock.com ® Photograph By David Messent/Photolibrary/Getty Images (bl) Image Source/Getty Images. 186 (l) Siede Preis/Photodisc/Getty Images (r) Tim Fitzharris/Minden Pictures. 187 FatCamera/

Getty Images (tc) wonderlandstock/Alamy Stock Photo (tr) Zoran Kompar Photography/Shutterstock (bl) Anitham Raju Yaragorla/Shutterstock (bc) Radius Images/Getty Images. 188 DARLYNE A. MURAWSKI/National Geographic Image Collection. 189 Brian Lasenby/Shutterstock.com. 190 (tl) Shchipkova Elena/Shutterstock.com (tc) IriGri/Shutterstock.com (tr) OlesyaNickolaeva/Shutterstock.com (bcl) HF media art/Shutterstock.com (bcr) kosmonova/Shutterstock.com (bl) zandyz/Shutterstock.com (br) Spiroview Inc/Shutterstock.com. 191 Agatha Kadar/Shutterstock.com. 192 (inset) Jabruson/Nature Picture Library. 194–195 Jabruson/Nature Picture Library. 196 (l) Jabruson/Nature Picture Library (tr) guichaoua/Alamy Stock Photo (br) Biosphoto/Superstock. 197 (l) Gleb Ivanov/Dreamstime.com (tr) Fuse/Corbis/Getty Images (cr) dezy/Shutterstock.com (br) pandapaw/Shutterstock.com. 198 (tl) James H Robinson/Oxford Scientific/Getty Images (tr) Jabruson/Nature Picture Library (b) Marius Hepp/EyeEm/Getty Images. 199 Jabruson/naturepl.com. 200 Randy Olson/National Geographic Image Collection. 201 André Quillien/Alamy Stock Photo. 202 AP Images/RICCARDO GANGALE. 203 The Goldman Environmental Prize. 204 Randy Olson/Getty Images. 205 Valeriya Anufriyeva/Shutterstock.com. 206 (t) Jabruson/Nature Picture Library. 208 Beyza Sultan DURNA/iStock/Getty Images. 209–211 khlongwangchao/Shutterstock.com. 210 (l) Okapi Conservation Project (r) Okapi Conservation Project. 211 Randy Olson/National Geographic Image Collection. 212 Jabruson/Nature Picture Library. 218 Ami Vitale. 219 Billion Photos/Shutterstock.com. 220–221 David Madison/Getty Images. 223 Bill Aron/PhotoEdit. 225 (tl) Inc/Shutterstock.com (tc) JONG KIAM SOON/Shutterstock.com (tr) Brand X Pictures/Stockbyte/Getty Images (bl) Jose Luis Pelaez Inc/Blend Images/Getty Images (bc) happyborder/iStock/Getty Images. 228 (tl) Andre Kleynhans/Shutterstock.com (tr) Kurit afshen/Shutterstock.com (cl) astudio/Shutterstock.com (cr) drawkman/Shutterstock.com (bl) Dave Primov/Shutterstock.com (br) Kurit Afshen/Shutterstock.com. 229 Page Light Studios/Shutterstock. 245 (t) Romiana Lee/Shutterstock.com (b) Rujipart/Shutterstock.com. 248 Norman Chan/Shutterstock.com. 254 JW LTD/Getty Images. 255 (tl) oticki/Shutterstock.com (cr) galdzer/iStock/Getty Images (bl) Siegfried Layda/Shutterstock (br) James P. Blair/National Geographic Image Collection. 257 (tl) Rob Marmion/Shutterstock.com (tc) koosverhagen/Getty Images (bl) Tetra Images/Getty Images (br) Lucie Danninger/Shutterstock.com. 260 (tl) Valeriya Pavlova/Shutterstock.com (tc) LittlePigPower/Shutterstock.com (tr) Sergey Nivens/Shutterstock.com (cl) Alina Cardiae Photography/Shutterstock.com (cr) urfin/Shutterstock.com (bl) rck_953/Shutterstock.com (br) Sergey Nivens/Shutterstock.com. 261 tupaiterbang/Shutterstock.com. 262–263 Bohemian Nomad Picturemakers/Corbis Documentary/Getty Images. 265 Rhett A. Butler/Mongabay.com. 266 (l) REBECCA HALE/National Geographic Image Collection. 266–267 Ligia Botero/Photodisc/Getty Images. 268 (l) bedo/iStock/Getty Images (r) Guenter Fischer/imageBROKER/Getty Images. 269 (l) REBECCA HALE/National Geographic Image Collection (r) REBECCA HALE/National Geographic Image Collection. 270–271 Lamberto Scipioni/Keystone RM/AGE Fotostock. 271 (c) Mark Moffett/Minden Pictures/Getty Images (r) valzan/Shutterstock.com. 272 Carlos Alkmin/Getty Images. 273 (t) Fernanda Preto/Alamy Stock Photo (b) DESIGNFACTS/Shutterstock.com. 274 REBECCA HALE/National Geographic Image Collection. 276 Aron Brand/Shutterstock.com. 288 David Madison/Getty Images. 289 (t) vovk 12/Shutterstock.com (b) iStock.com/MichaelDeLeon. 290 Ariel Skelley/DigitalVision/Getty Images. 291 (t) Inc/Shutterstock.com (tc) David Buffington/Photodisc/Getty Images (tr) BradWynnyk/iStock/Getty Images (cl) Leland Bobbe/Photodisc/Getty Images (c)

Acknowledgments

The Authors and Publisher would like to thank the following reviewers and teaching professionals for their valuable feedback during the development of the series.

Literature Reviewers

Carmen Agra Deedy, Grace Lin, Jonda C. McNair, Anastasia Suen

Global Reviewers

USA/Canada:

Kristin Blathras, Lead Literacy Teacher, Donald Morrill Elementary School, Chicago, IL; **Anna Ciani,** ESL Teacher, PS 291, Bronx, NY; **Jonathan Eversoll,** International Baccalaureate Curriculum Coach, Park Center Senior High, Brooklyn Park, MN; **Barbara A. Genovese-Fraracci,** District Program Specialist, Hacienda La Puente Unified School District, Hacienda Heights, CA; **Vanessa Gonzalez,** ESL Teacher/ESL Specialist, Rhoads Elementary, Katy, TX; **Leonila Izaguirre,** Bilingual-ESL Director, Pharr-San Juan-Alamo Independent School District, Pharr, TX; **Myra Junyk,** Literacy Consultant, Toronto, ON; **Susan Mayberger,** Coordinator of ESL, Migrant and Refugee Education, Omaha Public Schools, Omaha, NE; **Stephanie Savage Cantu,** Bilingual Teacher, Stonewall Jackson Elementary School, Dallas, TX; **Annette Torres Elias,** Consultant, Plano, TX; **Sonia James Upton,** ELL Consultant, Title III, Kentucky Department of Education, Frankfort, KY

Asia:

Mohan Aiyer, School Principal, Brainworks International School, Yangon; **Andrew Chuang,** Weige Primary School, Taipei; **Sherefa Dickson,** Head Teacher, SMIC, Beijing; **Ms Hien,** IP Manager, IPS Vietnam, Ho Chi Minh; **Christine Huang,** Principal, The International Bilingual School at the Hsinchu Science Park (IBSH), Hsinchu; **Julie Hwang,** Academic Consultant, Seoul; **David Kwok,** CEO, Englit Enterprise, Guangzhou; **Emily Li,** Teaching Assistant, SMIC, Beijing; **Warren Martin,** English Teacher, Houhai English, Beijing; **Bongse Memba,** Academic Coordinator, SMIC, Beijing; **Hoai Minh Nguyen,** Wellspring International Bilingual School, Ho Chi Minh; **Mark Robertson,** Elementary School Principal, Yangon Academy, Yangon; **Daphne Tseng,** American Eagle Institute, Hsinchu; **Amanda Xu,** Director of Teaching and Research, Englit Enterprise, Guangzhou; **Alice Yamamoto,** ALT, PL Gakuen Elementary School, Osaka; **Yan Yang,** Director of Research Development, Houhai English, Beijing

Middle East:

Lisa Olsen, Teacher, GEMS World Academy, Dubai, United Arab Emirates; **Erin Witthoft,** Curriculum Coordinator, Universal American School, Kuwait

Latin America:

Federico Brull, Academic Director, Cambridge School of Monterrey, Mexico; **Elizabeth Caballero,** English Coordinator, Ramiro Kolbe Campus Otay, Mexico; **Renata Callipo,** Teacher, CEI Romualdo, Brazil; **Lilia Huerta,** General Supervisor, Ramiro Kolbe Campus Presidentes, Mexico; **Rosalba Millán,** English Coordinator Primary, Instituto Cenca, Mexico; **Ann Marie Moreira,** Academic Consultant, Brazil; **Raúl Rivera,** English Coordinator, Ramiro Kolbe Campus Santa Fe, Mexico; **Leonardo Xavier,** Teacher, CEI Romualdo, Brazil

The Publisher gratefully acknowledges the contributions of the following National Geographic Explorers to our program and planet:

Joseph Lekuton, Zeb Hogan, Corneille Ewango, Cid Simões and Paola Segura